The Ninth Child

Lisa May LeBlanc

Siretona
CREATIVE

The Ninth Child
Lisa May LeBlanc
Calgary, Alberta, Canada
https://lisamayleblanc.com/

Published by Siretona Creative
Calgary, Alberta, Canada
https://siretona.com

Cover painting by Kyla Ferrier
Cover design, interior layout, and photo restorations by Travis Williams

Ebook: 978-1-988983-81-3
Trade paperback: 978-1-988983-80-6
Distributed to the trade by Ingram Book Company

Deluxe edition soft cover: 978-1-988983-82-0
Printed in Canada on 100% recycled FSC certified paper

For my nieces and nephews. Keep asking questions—
you deserve to know the answers.

And to Steve—you are my safe place.

Contents

Foreword vii

Introduction xi

1. Why I'm the youngest 1

2. The Farm 5

3. Don't Make Mom Mad 11

4. The Day My Brain Broke 15

5. Summertime 21

6. Becoming Auntie Lisa 25

7. Shenanigans 27

8. Only Child 29

9. My Favorite Uncle 39

10. College Girl 45

11. Falling In Love 51

12. Mono and the Big Breakup 57

13. I Dated a Townie 61

14. Fun Facts about Cult College 63

15. DVBS Tour 67

16. Wedding Plans and Campus Conflict 75

17. Calling Out Corruption 81

18. The Wedding 87

19. Newlywed Bliss and Bats 91

20. Remembering 97

21. Confronting My Parents 101

22. Moving to New Ulm 107

23. Moving to Winnipeg 111

24. My Parents' Origin Stories 117

25. Infertility 125

26. Adoption Options 131

27. Meeting the Birth Grandparents 135

28. Becoming Parents 139

29. Adoption #2 147

30. Separation and Reconciliation 151

31. Finding Hope and Healing 157

Epilogue 167

Acknowledgements 169

The Journey to the Cover Art 171

Questions for reflection and discussion 177

Photo Album 179

Foreword

WE ARE BORN PERFECT IN mind, body, and spirit, for we bear the likeness of God. At that first moment, we are without blemish. We are born into a world full of imperfection, exposed and vulnerable. That which happens to us afterwards, and how we respond, become a lifelong struggle as we strive to return to the perfection first gifted to us. We seek to recall God's love.

From a unique friendship and close family relationship, enriched through 30-plus years as Lisa embraced her role as Mom to our granddaughters in a loving, open adoption, comes my deep appreciation of her remarkable story.

This is a tale of a tireless witness to the power of belief in God's Word, and in the healing power of faith. It is a testament to the indomitable human spirit, struggling with early childhood trauma. Lisa's sincere determination to reach out to outcasts, to others faced with overpowering psycho-emotional challenges, resonates in her life and in these chapters. It serves to remind us that truly, God works through us, imperfect as we are, to help others in need.

Lisa's deeply personal revelation of her numerous difficult experiences touches the reader on so many levels, compelling us to understand the importance of being resilient and confident in the ability to overcome.

We emerge strengthened and ready to "fight the good fight." Lisa was and is a strong advocate for open adoption, and this message of unconditional love has impacted scores of young pregnant girls and their parents everywhere. Teens all arrive to a time in their growth that they question, refute, and rebel. To each parent, this is a time of frustration, doubt, and considerable dismay. How does one cope when there is a crisis in communication? What does one do when the core family values and beliefs are threatened? To whom does a parent turn when those very foundations are themselves weakened from an assault long before they are questioned by your own angry teenager child?

The reader will easily identify with Lisa's very human talk with God that resonates with our own troubled times when all sense and hope is missing.

No one has an infallible approach to parenting, neither for the first nor the next child-adult. Yet, in Lisa's account, there is hope and truth that has served her family well, and will continue to be a bedrock reference for the reader.

I have truly been quite eager to read Lisa's testimony of survival and growth as she has shared so much with her openness and generosity throughout the years. The topic is especially interesting to me following my own enquiry into healing in my research for my Master's in Counseling. My published thesis, *Searching For The Connection: A Narrative Enquiry Into The Healing Process* (B.U., 1999), proposed that healing is facilitated when all three human essences of the individual—mind, body, and spirit—are brought into balance. During my research, my clients presented many issues that responded well to this therapy, and I am delighted to sense additional affirmation is to be enjoyed in Lisa's account, in which these fundamental connections are restored. I recall noting that it was the renowned physician Carl Jung who remarked that, while a clinical diagnosis is important, "the crucial thing is the story. For it alone shows the human background and the human suffering. Only at that point can the doctor's therapy begin to operate."

We are swept up in Lisa's story as it gently unfolds in a calm pastoral setting. Storytelling is at its best when everyone can relate, and we appreciate glimpses of our own childhood. Like Lisa, we do not foresee the approaching clouds, the storm that will forever mar this idyllic time.

The Ninth Child appeals to the reader from the very first page, for it refuses to stay in the darkness of continuous trial and tribulations that, while they are indeed there to discourage life itself, the heroine heaves herself up from the turbulence of her mind and soul battle to claim her rightful place in this confusing world.

Must we, like Lisa, shout at God as we cry in frustration and helplessness? Does He actually answer our soul-felt questions? The reader will discover essential wisdom in these chapters and importantly, an affirmation that God seeks communication with us, that His answers come to us in those moments of our greatest brokenness. Prayer is powerful.

Does the world end when something real bad happens to you? No. Read this story and you will see that there is still goodness and hope to be enjoyed as you heal from that hurtful time. To know this is to be empowered, for it leads to understanding and compassion—Divine gifts that are there to embrace and to share.

As a married father of three adult children, grandfather of 9, and now retired from 40 years as a teacher, I read Lisa's *The Ninth Child* with a wish that I'd had the benefit of a good dose of the wisdom seeping from these insights, but I also sense a great anticipation that in my own future writing efforts, I shall be inspired to pay it forward.

Enjoy the read.

Roméo Lemieux, B.Ed. M.Ed. (Counseling)
Author of: *Searching For The Connection: A Narrative Enquiry Into The Healing Process* (Brandon University, 1999) *Incognito* (Pearson Ed, 2004), *Right Side UP Side Down* (FriesenPress, 2014).

Introduction

GOD AND I HAD BEEN having conversations about writing this book for several years. It began when someone else shared their trauma story. A whisper echoed in my heart: "You have a story, too." Over time this whisper became louder, more insistent, and downright obnoxious. It demanded courageous vulnerability. It wasn't shutting up, so I made a deal with God.

"OK, God—I will write my story, but there is no way I can do that until both of my parents are gone, because there is no context in which they would read my story and not feel disrespected and betrayed. They don't recognize these events in my life as trauma. They don't understand how talking about trauma brings it out of the dark into the light and offers an opportunity for healing. I'm not going to hurt them this way. Once they are both gone, we can talk about this again."

The voice quieted, and I accepted that as God's agreement. Until 2019, when the whispers began again. By early 2020, the argument was again in full swing. I was sitting on the couch during a pandemic lockdown, doomscrolling my social media in an attempt to ignore the voice in my head. It didn't work. I decided to step into the fight. It wasn't the first time I threw it down with God, and it won't be the last. It went something like this ...

ME: OK God, say I write the stupid book which is probably going to be crap and no one will want to read it anyway and I'll be stuck with boxes full of books in my basement that someone else is going to have to cart off to the dump when I die—I mean, I know nothing about publishing! How am I supposed to even do that? Like is there even a publisher right here in my neighborhood who would even be interested in looking at it, let alone publishing it?? C'mon! You know what? I'll prove it to you. I just downloaded the handy little Nextdoor.ca app on my phone, so I'm going to search for a publisher right here in Cranston, Calgary ...

And there she was. Colleen McCubbin of Siretona Creative. A boutique publisher right here in my own neighborhood. Except I wasn't done with my bratty rant-fest.

STILL ME: Is she even a Christian and would she understand the culture I come from? And she's probably awesome and I'll like her and we might become friends and she's going to like my writing and want to publish my book. Right??

GOD: Yup.

ME: So, I guess I'm doing this thing.

GOD: I'll help. Are you done being a brat now?

ME: Yup.

I reached out to Colleen. She read my blog and set up a phone consult with me. She gave me the encouragement I needed to start putting words on a page. But fear wasn't done with me yet.

Why am I even doing this? Vulnerability is terrifying. Why am I putting myself through this? Writing this book will likely end relationships with some people. Does my story even matter?

Yes, it does. Story allows us to see the world through someone else's point of view. Perspective is a powerful thing. It's why I love things like binoculars and kaleidoscopes.

Here's the biggest reason I wrote this book: telling my trauma/healing story might help you unlock a piece of your story and access another level of healing. That's what other people's stories have done for me, and that's what I want to do for you.

Maybe you don't have a trauma story. Lucky you. If my story helps grow your empathy for other people's trauma stories, that's a win. Our world needs a great deal more empathy and it is my pleasure to contribute to that very worthy endeavor. If you are offended by my story and don't like me anymore, I'm okay with that. Telling the truth is worth the risk.

1

Why I'm the youngest

THE WORLD WAS FILLED WITH unspeakable beauty the day my brain broke.

The late springtime sun shone warm on my thin, small shoulders.

The sky was a perfect robin's egg blue.

The breeze was warm and sweet with the scent of new grass and flowers bursting into bloom.

My new summer socks were blindingly white and perfect. They didn't have the lace trim I wanted—those were too expensive. Still, just looking down at my little ankles encased in a gentle hug of perfect whiteness made me smile.

Soon, that perfect clean whiteness would be a dim memory.

So would my smile.

I was born in 1964, the ninth and final child of my parents. Six girls, three boys. My dad was a dairy farmer. Dad believed in raising the help rather than hiring it. He also believed in the Holy Spirit method of birth control. If God didn't want them to have any more kids, they wouldn't. The result was eight children born in ten years, all single births. Four years later I appeared. My poor mom.

According to Mom, I never went to my first well-baby checkup. Doc Carlson called my mom, and as I understand it, the conversation went something like this:

DOC: How are you doing? How's the baby?

MOM: Fine

DOC: No need to bring the baby in for a checkup, but I want to see your husband. Send him in for the appointment instead.

Dad complied with the request and went to the clinic to see Doc. Their conversation was mostly one-sided, and it went something like this:

DOC: I know you have strong religious beliefs about birth control. I don't care. Unless you want to raise ten children on your own, the tenth being a newborn, you will take this prescription for birth control pills next door to the pharmacist and get it filled today, and your wife will begin taking them tomorrow, because she won't survive another birth.

Dad went to the pharmacy, Mom started taking the pill, and I remained the youngest.

While the sheer number of people in the home sometimes overwhelmed me, I benefited from having so many older siblings. There was always a playmate, someone to read to me, and a lap to sit on while the family gathered around the grainy black & white TV to watch *Petticoat Junction*. It aired every Saturday night after chores, milking the cows, and pancakes.

There were more kids than seating in front of the TV, so there were usually a couple of kids sprawled out on the floor. One of my siblings was fond of watching TV while they lay on their stomach, allowing me to sit on their back along with my Teddy and Blankie. Of course, this privilege was denied if I started bouncing up and down on their back. I didn't learn to sit still in church—I learned to sit still in front of *Petticoat Junction*.

My family enjoys a deep legacy of faith in God. I remember our home filled with teens after church on a Sunday night for "Singspiration." Once a month the teens and young adults would gather at someone's home after Sunday night service. A simple buffet-style meal would be served. Hymns and choruses would be sung, a group game would be played, and everyone would eat and visit until it was time to go home. Every few months it was our turn to host.

My elementary school-aged siblings resented me a great deal on those nights. They had to go to bed while I stayed up being passed from lap to lap. I

I felt an overwhelming sense of love. I felt protected. I felt singled out and special.

---

enjoyed their resentment, probably a bit too much, even at the tender age of two.

I remember Dad putting me in my crib after one such evening. I had my ducky blanket but I forgot my teddy bear. He went downstairs to get it, came back to tuck me in and smiled as he said goodnight. Later that night I woke up to moonlight streaming in my window—brighter than I had ever seen before. I stood up in my crib and leaned over the rail to better see out the window. I could see the farmyard, the tractors in the driveway, and the barn. I looked up into the clouds above the milk house, and there He was.

God was smiling at me. I felt an overwhelming sense of love. I felt protected. I felt singled out and special.

I thought I must be dreaming so I laid down, scrunched my eyes shut, and popped back up only to find He was still there. "Hi God," I said. His eyes twinkled at me. I laid down and went back to sleep feeling a warmth and love I couldn't express or understand.

Obviously, no one believes a toddler when she announces she saw God, but I have never forgotten that encounter. Looking back, I am grateful for it as I would draw comfort from that memory more than once.

2

The Farm

A DAIRY FARM IS A thing of wonder. There are gardens and crops that need tending. There is always new life that needs nurturing. Everyone has a job to do regardless of age or gender. A family farm requires many strong backs and willing hands pitching in to do their part for the farm to run well. This is true of a dairy farm especially, as cows need milking every twelve hours no matter what. The cows don't care if it's raining or snowing, or if you are sick or tired or injured. They need scheduled milking, and to neglect that job is to jeopardize the health of the herd and the entire dairy operation.

As the youngest in the family, my job was to look after the farm babies. As a young girl that meant keeping track of the farm cats, most of whom were feral. A few of them were tamer than the others and kept to our farm, while the wild ones would migrate back and forth between our farm and our neighbors.

The feral cats who traveled around were the smart ones. The cats we were able to tame stuck around and were the unwitting victims of childhood shenanigans, including getting dressed in doll clothes and pushed around the yard in an old moldy pram. The unluckiest cats ended up getting baptised by immersion. That also meant arms full of cat scratches, but it was a risk worth taking to make sure our cats were good Baptists.

Healthy cats are important to a dairy farm. They control the rodent population to protect the stored grains which feed the cows. I paid attention to which cats were pregnant. When they were skinny again, it was time for one of my favorite tasks—hunting for the new kittens.

A smart momma cat would make her way into the hayloft above the milking barn, make a nest in a back corner of the loft, and settle in to birth and nurse her kittens. This is where I usually found the new litters. I would count the kittens, check to see if they looked healthy by their coat quality and weight gain. I would carefully inspect their eyes for discharge. Eye infections in new kittens were common. Once their eyes began to open, they had little defense against the copious amounts of dust that exists in a barn loft filled with haybales.

When I found a litter with infected eyes, I would scoop them up into a rag-lined box and bring them to the back entry of the house. I made sure momma cat followed me so she knew where they were and could continue to nurse them. Momma cat was treated to extra table scraps and saucers of creamy milk while her babies were under my care.

This was as far as any animal ever got into the house. Mom made it clear that animals belonged outside. The dog and cats may be considered pets, but they were still working animals and belonged outside where they could do their jobs. She already had nine kids creating havoc in the house—the last thing she needed was cleaning up after animals as well.

Over the next few days, I would treat their eyes with a special solution made from boric acid, using a clean cloth to saturate the eye and clean away the discharge. When the infection cleared up, I would put the box outside for momma cat to carry her kittens back to whatever new nest she'd made, since I had found and invaded the last one.

I would continue to monitor the litter to see if they all survived and remained healthy. We had a few tom cats rotating between neighboring farms and they were rarely friendly. They would sometimes attack and kill the new kittens. Dad said it was the tom cats' instinct to thin out future competition, as well as nature's way of ensuring the strongest survive. Farm kids simply accepted these kinds of things as part of the circle of life.

The farm dog was a critical part of running a dairy farm. Our farm dogs were always Rough Collies, and they were always named Prince or Princess. I don't know why—I wish I had thought to ask Dad before he passed away. I recently learned that when he was growing up he had a dog named King. That may be where the royal names originated.

Collies are wonderful herd dogs with a strong protective nature, especially toward children. They are smart and easy to train due to their innate herding skills and a desire to please their people.

When I was a toddler, Princess came to our family as a puppy. Dad was a good trainer. He took her to the barn with him during milking. Princess was initially afraid of the huge black and white giants with quick hooves and long swishing tails. Dad let the puppy explore at her own pace. After a few days, the fear subsided and curiosity took over. Then the training began. Dad took Princess to the feed lot where he would round up the cows into the pole barn connected to the milking barn. Then he would open the door to the barn and the cows would file in, each to their own spot. It didn't take long for Princess to catch on. Soon she was doing the herding on her own.

The bond between Princess and Dad was amazing to see. Princess knew her job and did it very well. She slept outside my parents' bedroom window, waiting to hear Dad's 4 am alarm. She raced to the feedlot to herd the cows into the pole barn. By the time Dad got to the barn, all he had to do was open the door and the cows filed in, each to their own stanchion.

In the afternoon this routine was repeated. Princess waited outside the kitchen window while Dad had his cookies and milk. She would stare at the window, waiting to see Dad's hand pointing toward the barn. Then she would take off like a shot, racing to the feedlot to herd the cows back into the pole barn.

Princess had her own language. She knew the neighbors and had a different bark for each of them, announcing who was driving past the farm. She had a specific bark for the vet and another one for salesmen. Family and visitors were announced with even more excitement. Her most excited greeting was reserved for my dad. Princess would wag her tail so hard her whole body would sway back and forth. Dad would talk to her and pet her, and she would have the biggest grin on her face. I have never seen a dog grin like that since.

The bark we knew best was the loud, sharp "cows are out!" bark in the middle of the night. We were jolted out of our sleep by that bark. No one needed to be told—we all jumped out of bed and ran outside to round up the cows and get them back in the feedlot. That's when I witnessed Princess at the top of her game. She was a wonder to behold—staring down a stubborn cow, turning it around, and forcefully herding it back where it belonged with sharp barks and well-placed nips. I learned from her how to anticipate and cut off a cow's escape and get it going in the right direction again.

I had a strong bond with Princess too, more so than my siblings. She was a puppy when I was a baby. By the time I was two, she claimed me as her puppy and she was very protective of me. She would stand by the car when the family arrived home from church, waiting for me. Dad would put me on her back and keep me steady while I rode Princess to the house.

Even when I was a toddler, Mom would often let me play outside on my own because she knew Princess would look after me. Mom kept an eye on me to be sure, as she was outdoors regularly to tend the washing line and the gardens, but the constant supervision was provided by the dog.

There was no need for a fence to keep me in the yard—Princess was my nanny. With a yard full of tractors and farm implements that spelled death or dismemberment to an unsupervised toddler, Princess walked circles around me, herding me as I explored the yard and picked dandelions. She never let me take one step off the grass. She refused to let me anywhere near the road or the driveway. When I got tired and plopped down on the grass, she would lay down beside me. I remember laying on top of her and going to sleep—she didn't move until I woke up again.

Mom once told me about the time she called me into the house for lunch and I didn't want to come in. I wanted to stay outside with Princess. Mom came outside with a wooden spoon in her hand to encourage me to obey.

Unbeknownst to everyone, evil lurked in our small, seemingly idyllic community.

Princess took one look at that spoon, placed herself between me and my mother, and snarled. Her ears went flat. She lowered her head, bared her teeth, and leveled a glare at my mother that made her back slowly into the house. There was no way Mom was going to fight the dog for me—the dog would win. My lunch waited until I was ready to come inside.

These and many more happy experiences in my early childhood convinced me that I was loved. I was cared for. I felt safe and secure. I had a role and I belonged in the family.

It didn't take long for that to change. Unbeknownst to everyone, evil lurked in our small, seemingly idyllic community. When I was six my world tilted. My brain broke. Everything changed.

3

Don't Make Mom Mad

BEFORE LONG I GREW OUT of adorable and into annoying. I think it was my coping mechanism for feeling left out. It was obvious that my older siblings all had a special connection that stopped just short of me. The age difference is the easy answer, and maybe that's all it was in the beginning, but nonetheless I always felt I was on the outside looking in.

The only explanation given by select siblings at the time was that they didn't want me. A few reasons were offered, the most popular being that the police dropped me off as a baby and threatened to arrest the whole family if they didn't keep me. I knew this story wasn't true, but it was true that I felt unwanted, and repeated comments like that reinforced that core belief.

This is the kind of banter that older sibs subject the youngest to all the time, but for whatever reason, my feelings were easily hurt. That seemed to be my siblings' main complaint—I was too sensitive. It also made me an easy target. Maybe they thought they were doing me a favor by trying to toughen me up.

I knew better than to fight back when unkind things were said, and when I was called names, but I was only willing to take so much before I sought retribution. Conflict happened often, frequently noisy and ending up with me crying, which typically resulted in me being told to shut up. I learned that my reaction was the problem, not the unkindness that caused me to react.

Even as a very young child I recognized when Mom was having a bad day. I learned quickly that the best strategy to get through the day was "don't make Mom mad."

One day I saw her alone in the kitchen after breakfast. She looked so tired, and the day had barely begun. I wanted to do something nice for her, lighten her load somehow. I decided to surprise her by making her bed. It was a big bed, and my little 6-year-old arms could only reach so far, but I did my best.

Just the slightest bit of attention was like a drop of water on a dried-up sponge.

I couldn't wait any longer for her to discover my surprise, so I went to the kitchen and told her I made her bed for her. She sighed and got up and went to the bedroom. She was not pleased.

"Don't help me," she said angrily. "All you do is make more work for me." She shoved me up against the wall at the foot of the bed. "If you want to know how to make a bed, just stand there and watch."

She tore off all the bedding down to the sheets and remade the bed, all the while berating my poor attempt to help her. I remember crying and apologizing. Now she was mad that I was crying. From then on, my best strategy for survival was withdrawing. Making myself as unnoticeable as possible. Spending time alone. Not offering any assistance. Quietly complying when I was told to do something. I wasn't very good at any of those things, but I tried.

I began to understand that safety came from staying out of the way and not making Mom mad. And definitely not crying when my feelings got hurt, because that was annoying.

I failed at not crying. I'm still a crier. My tender heart and emotional nature made me vulnerable. I was ripe for the picking by a predator. Just the slightest bit of attention was like a drop of water on a dried-up sponge.

4

The Day My Brain Broke

I WAS SIX YEARS OLD. There was a deacon in my parents' church whose three daughters had already left home, leaving just him and his wife. He worked as the local elementary school janitor. I overheard this couple being ridiculed on a regular basis in my home. There was something off about them. She seemed especially clueless.

But he was nice to me. He bypassed my siblings and smiled at only me. He would tweak my cheek and make a funny noise. For the first time I felt noticed as an individual, not just one of the pack. He made me feel special. He told me I looked pretty in my church dress. I had never been spoken to like this before. I had never felt noticed in a good way before. I didn't know I was being groomed by a predator. No one knew what that was.

So, when he asked if I would like to go home with him and his wife after church one day I begged my mom for permission. Could I please go with them and stay the afternoon? They would bring me back for church for the evening service. With a bunch of other kids to keep track of, a break from my conflicts with siblings would have been a tempting proposition. I imagine

15

that was an easy yes.

Before I was born it was a common occurrence for my grandparents and my then-teenage aunts to take one of the siblings home with them on Sundays after church, keeping track of whose turn it was to have that special privilege. This practice stopped when all the aunts grew up and left home, so I had never had that experience.

Pedophiles are smart. They look for patterns to exploit, and my molester was no different. He played on that familiar theme which made it easier to convince my parents that it would be okay for me to stay with him and his wife for the afternoon.

My world changed forever that day.

I walked home with the deacon and his wife—they only lived a few blocks from the church—my hand in his. We walked past an old house with peeling paint and a sagging front porch. The front yard was bordered by honeysuckle in full bloom. I can smell it even now—the air was heavy with the thick, sweet aroma.

We must have had lunch. I don't remember that part. I do remember her going upstairs to her bedroom for a nap while he settled in his chair to watch the football game.

There was a guitar standing in the corner by the TV. I was curious about it, never having seen one up close. He encouraged me to pick it up and try to play it. It was too big for me to hold on my own, so he picked me up and put me on his lap, helping me to position the guitar, showing me where to put my hands. Left hand on the fret. Right hand strumming the strings. His hand started wandering. His lap was suddenly very uncomfortable, no longer soft and yielding.

I was afraid of what was happening, but I was more afraid of getting in trouble for speaking or being rude. When it hurt, I found my courage.

Once I was able to escape, I ran outside. I didn't even stop to put on my shoes. I ran down the back alley to the house at the end which belonged to my grandparents. I entered the back door and went up the stairs from the mudroom to the kitchen, where I stopped in my tracks. The house was silent. I knew they were napping. *How am I going to explain why I am standing here with no shoes on?*

So many thoughts careened wildly through my mind:

I don't know how to answer that question.

I can't tell them what happened—I don't know words for that.

I am afraid to say a bad thing about a man from church—I will get in trouble.

I am afraid they will think I'm a bad girl. They can never know how bad I am.

There is no safe place for me. Not Grandma's house. Not home. Not church.

I was out of options. I knew my only choice was to go back to his house. I heard a snap in my brain at the very top of my head, kind of like a too-taut rubber band breaking.

I turned around, left their house, and went back to his house. I hid under the big weeping willow tree in the front yard, embraced by the long tendrils of leaves cascading down from the branches. He seemed relieved that I had returned. He sat on the front step, coaxing me to come back in the house. I stayed under the tree, practically hugging the trunk, until his wife got up from her nap. With her awake he couldn't do anything else to me.

She came outside to see what was going on. "Aren't you silly, going outside in your socks," she said to me. "Come inside the house, dear." I followed her into the house and curled into a fetal position on their couch with my back to the room. He came and knelt behind me. I felt his hot breath on the back of my neck as he begged me not to tell my dad or my grandpa—he seemed terrified at the idea of them finding out what he had done. He said he was sorry.

My brain was already broken. I was unable to process anything he was saying at that point. I said there was nothing to forgive because nothing happened. I repeated over and over again, "It didn't happen, it didn't happen, it didn't happen."

When his wife started making sandwiches for supper, I stuck to her side like glue. I never let her out of my sight for the rest of the afternoon. She thought I was cute for wanting to know how she made sandwiches.

We sat at the table, ate the sandwiches, and walked back to church for the evening service. I sat in the family pew. I sang the hymns. I sat quietly during the sermon. No one asked me how my afternoon was. There was no "Did you have a nice time?" or "What did you do?" There was no reference made at all that I had been somewhere else for the afternoon. It didn't matter. No one cared. My self-esteem plummeted that day and stayed low most of my life.

When we returned home after church my mom discovered my ruined socks. My brand new, never-been-worn-before, sparkling white, summer church socks. Except they weren't white anymore. They would never be white again. As Mom yelled at me and put me over her knee for a spanking, I realized neither would I.

I tried to put it out of my mind. When the memory threatened to overtake me, I would run to my room, curl up with my teddy bear in the corner and chant, "It didn't happen it didn't happen it didn't happen." This dissociation and self-soothing chanting went on for a few years. Somehow, I went to church three times a week and shook this man's hand with a smile on my face. I watched him serve communion to my parents. And I never said a word.

Until one day, two years later, it all came spilling out.

Mom and I were in town for some reason.

On our way out of town to go back home we drove past his street. I told Mom I didn't like that man. "Why would you say such a thing?" I still had no words for what happened to me. But somehow, I found my voice, and told her that he had touched me.

My brain did some pretty amazing acrobatic maneuvers that day, as brains do to protect us from trauma that can't be processed. Sometimes the brain will create a false memory that makes more sense to our current experiences than the truth does.

I remember standing in the kitchen and telling Mom the whole story. She looked at me and said, "I don't have time for this, I have to finish the laundry." She walked away.

I would later learn that my memory of this event was wrong, but until I realized that, every time I replayed that memory, for all the years I was growing up, I truly believed she had walked away from me.

You think children don't think about suicide? Think again.

My soul shattered. My heart hurt so badly I thought I might die. I wished for death. This memory supported what I already knew to be true of my siblings, but I had still held out hope that Mom loved me.

Nope.

It would be better if I was dead. If I died, they would be happy and I wouldn't hurt anymore. Thus began my suicide ideation.

You think children don't think about suicide? Think again. It became a major part of my thought life for my whole life. Day after day, waking up in the morning, regretting the fact that I was still alive.

5

Summertime

BEES BUZZ, BIRDS SING. THE farm comes alive with a gasping breath of fresh air and new promise.

Shoes are forgotten as a fresh carpet of grass thickens in the yard. The day grows long and longer still. The nights are soft and friendly.

There is time for an occasional game of evening softball, until the sun goes down and the yard light comes on.

The swimming hole beckons.

Grandpa arrives with his ice cream maker.

And, Bible camp. I am forever grateful to my parents that they made summer Bible camp a priority for me. Some of my best friends and confidantes were made at summer camp. My deepest moments with God happened at summer camp. One sip of Orange Crush and I'm there again.

Lake Shetek in southern Minnesota. Quaint log cabins. Walking to the lake with my cabin mates to swim every afternoon, a threadbare towel slung over my thin shoulders. I even enjoyed daily chapel. The sermons were crafted for kids, so they were far more interesting than regular sermons at home.

I was so excited to go to camp that I would start packing two weeks before. But then I needed to wear the clothes I packed, so had to unpack and repack a few times before it was actually time to go. I counted the days and then the hours. It was a magical five days free from yelling, slapping, shoving, and hiding in my room or riding my bike to the cottonwood tree down the road to get away from the abuse for awhile.

I encountered God in a new way at camp. All distractions were stripped away. God had a clear path to my heart. I felt His love wash over me all over again, just like I had in my crib that night when I saw God. I knew He saw me, He loved me, and someday it would all be okay. I was safe.

I met new kids who actually wanted to be my friend. Back then all we had was snail mail. We exchanged addresses and promised to write.

The week ended far too soon. Friday night, the last night at camp, was awful. I would cry myself to sleep, not wanting to go home. I had a camp counselor who noticed and cared. She took me into her room and asked a few questions. It all came out—the abuse and bullying I was suffering at home. I didn't want to go back. Couldn't she find a way for me to go somewhere else? Anywhere else had to be better than what I was going home to. Of course, no such options existed.

She knew my parents. She was shocked. I don't know how much of my story she believed, but she was kind and made me feel heard. That was certainly more compassion than I was used to. She comforted me the best she could and tucked me into my bunk.

When I got home all I could do was cry. My chest hurt. My stomach was tight. I was scared of being home and of what I was feeling in that moment. Mom told me to get over it and stop being so dramatic.

No one knew what a panic attack was back then. I was once again in a place where there was no safe place for me. And I had several years of survival in front of me until I could leave and make my own safe place.

Fear and anxiety created thoughts that relentlessly circled my brain:

There is more than this. There must *be more than this.*

If there isn't more than this what is the point of it all?

I can't see more than this.

God, can you see more than this for me? I remember you smiled at me in my crib. Are you still smiling at me?

A tiny flicker of hope.

It didn't last long, but I found ways to cope by spending as much time alone as I could, withdrawing into my mind by reading books and doing puzzles.

The mailbox became my best friend. Letters from my pen pal brought me back to that calm confidence I felt at camp. I was reminded someone liked me enough to take the time to write a letter and spend eight cents on a stamp to send it to me. The hope of the next letter arriving from my pen pal got me through some pretty bad moments.

Moments when I would sit on the steps by the back door of the farmhouse and stare at my dad's shotguns. Trying to figure out how to take one and position it just right. My arms weren't long enough to reach the trigger. How could I rig something up so I could pull a string to pull the trigger? I was good at puzzles, but this was one puzzle I couldn't solve.

The mail would come and sometimes there was a letter for me. I thought how hurt and disappointed my friend would be if I stopped writing to her and didn't go to camp next summer because I was dead. I took the letter to my room to read, immediately getting out my kitten stationery pad to write back. And the dark demons of death were pushed back one more time.

There were still good things happening. Everything that occurred from day to day was experienced through a filter of fear and anxiety and depression, but there was still laughter and joy in my home.

There is no bold line of delineation between good and evil, chaos and calm, abuse and nurture. All these things can exist in the same space, creating a kind of inexplicable tension. There are layers of joy, sadness, pain, comfort, safety, and insecurity, and they can all fuse together.

Just when I felt calm and stable, something would happen to make Mom mad, and the storm of chaos and uncertainty would roll in, creating an emotional fog that was very difficult to navigate.

6

Becoming Auntie Lisa

A MARVELOUS THING HAPPENED JUST before I turned eleven. I became Auntie Lisa. I was so excited! I loved babies. I was counting the days until I was old enough to babysit for the neighbors.

My first nephew who made me an aunt was born a couple hours away, so I got to see him every few months. I was my sister's constant shadow, waiting for the chance to hold him, count his tiny fingers, and kiss his sweet face.

I was Auntie Lisa. At long last, I had found my place in the family.

Soon after my nephew's birth, my first niece was born in Georgia. While I knew I wouldn't be able to meet her right away, I already felt a fierce love for her. I also knew this was just the beginning—the happy invasion of the next generation had just gotten started.

Being an aunt was my favorite thing in the world. When sibs came to the farm for the weekend, I was ready to take that baby off their hands as much and often as I was allowed. I woke up for nighttime bottles and diaper changes. I sat and played with them for hours. I oversaw bath time whenever I got the chance. I claimed them from the church nursery after Sunday service.

As they grew older, there was a whole farm to explore and I was a willing tour guide. Cows and calves to see. Kittens to find. A hayloft to play in. Snowmen to build. As they grew older still, there were makeup lessons. Flute lessons. Sewing Barbie doll clothes together. Talking about what they wanted to be when they grew up. The nephews mostly abandoned me by the time they were teens to embrace more manly pursuits, but the nieces and I had lots to do together.

Just down the road on a nearby farm were two nephews and a niece. I got to see them a lot. Before my niece was born and the boys were quite small, Mom and I would occasionally bring them along to the shopping mall about 30 minutes away. I found it amusing to observe other ladies frowning at teenage girls with babies. I deliberately made excuses to push the cart with my little nephew around the mall just to smile at the scowlers. I moved my ring to my left hand and turned it backwards just to confuse them even more.

I was Auntie Lisa. At long last, I had found my place in the family.

7

Shenanigans

ONE EVENING AFTER SUPPER WE girls were doing the dishes. I must have been around age ten or eleven. Dad always showered after milking the cows before he came to the supper table, so I don't remember why he decided to shower after supper. Maybe the milking had gone late and he didn't have time to shower before supper?

Despite Mom's half-hearted protests and giggles, he convinced her to join him in the basement for a shower. She was blushing as he led her past all us kids through the kitchen and down the stairs. She was blushing even more when they came back up!

Dad was not shy about his attraction to Mom. She would pass by his chair in the living room, and he'd reach out to touch her hand or pinch her bottom. I even witnessed a few laps around the dining room table, Dad chasing Mom, while she waved a dish towel in the air squealing "Gerritt! Not in front of the kids!" She would give up, let him catch her, and share a kiss.

I loved that my parents loved each other. Their displays of affection didn't embarrass me. On the contrary, it made me feel secure. In a world where divorce was becoming more common, I never once worried about my parents breaking up.

When I was old enough to drive, my dad gave me money to buy a Christmas gift from him to Mom. I found the sheerest, shortest, hot pink nightie available. The black lace and thong panty put it over the top. I put it in a box that had originally held a new Bible and wrapped it up to Mom from Dad. He didn't ask so I didn't tell.

On Christmas Eve as the gifts were being handed out and opened, I gave Dad the signal that Mom was opening his gift. She carefully removed the wrapping (save the paper for next year!), saw the Bible box, and muttered, "I don't need a new Bible."

She opened the box and let out a squeal like we had never heard before. She refused to display her gift for all to see. She questioned Dad as to when and where he would have purchased such a thing. He said, "I gave the money to Lisa. She's the one who bought it." He dissolved in laughter when she passed the box over to him to see. Of course he held it up, completing Mom's embarrassment! We all had a good laugh and she set it aside. "You better have kept the receipt, because that's going back to the store!" she laughed.

Later that night I could hear them whispering and giggling in their room. Dad had convinced her to try it on for him. I guess she had decided not to return it. In that moment I felt happy and safe, and all was right in my world.

The next Christmas, Mom wanted revenge. She gave me money to get Dad a present. A black speedo thong. The sibs didn't really get it, but Mom and Dad and I had a good laugh.

8

Only Child

HERE'S THE THING ABOUT BEING the youngest. Eventually everyone else moves out and it is just you. Wahoo!

I did the math. I formulated a plan. I would have four short years as an only child, and I intended to use them well. The status quo would be no longer. I was about to shake things up.

I was fourteen the day my next oldest sibling drove down the gravel road toward college. I stood with my parents in the kitchen, watching the diminishing dust cloud behind her car. I turned and smiled at them.

They looked at me and their faces morphed from a proud smile to exhaustion. Mom: "I'm tired. I need a nap." Dad: "Me too." I chuckled softly to myself. Take that nap—you are going to need it.

It began with unfettered conversation at the supper table. No one remained to tell me to be quiet or make me feel stupid. I found a cleverness and wit that I had never been able to exercise. Wonder of wonders—I could make them laugh!

Our church started its own Christian School, which opened the year I started grade eight. I was the only kid from our family to leave the public school and go to a private Christian school.

I didn't have many friends at public school, and I was feeling a lot of anxiety about junior high. Suddenly there were multiple classrooms instead of one homeroom. There were big lockers and kids making out in the hallway between classes. There were rude boys that would flip up my skirt and yell, "It's dress up day!" I was not enjoying myself. So, when I was given the option to go to school in the church basement where I felt confident and safe, I was all in.

We started with a whopping 13 kids who made up the entire student body. There was even a local news crew at the church, filming us filing into the side door of the church the first day of school. It was a short story and an even shorter film.

I was a little excited about my evening news debut. I had saved up some babysitting money and bought a new white eyelet lace top with puffy short sleeves. It had elastic to draw in the short sleeves, the scoop neck, and the waist. It was embroidered around the neckline with tiny flowers and green leaves. I wore it with a green skirt I had just sewn, and new brown leather clogs.

We sat at fold-out desks with dividers between us. These were called offices, built by my dad and a few other church men. We followed the ACE curriculum (Accelerated Christian Education), which is a self-taught method using workbooks called PACEs. We read the material ourselves and completed the quizzes and tests. If you failed the final test, you had to erase all the answers in the workbook and do the whole thing again.

I was an advanced reader, so the curriculum wasn't difficult for me, except for math. I hated math. I still hate math. The minute they handed me a PACE for algebra, I was done with all of it. I still see no reason whatsoever to mix up the alphabet with the numbers. For the love of God and all that is sane and reasonable, numbers and letters need to stay in their own lanes. My mind will not be changed about this.

Mom volunteered at school as the Reading Monitor. This provided us with a great number of shared experiences. I was an avid reader from the time I first learned to read. Under Mom's tutelage, I learned to speed read. As far as I know, my record of reading 1800 words per minute with 80% or better comprehension was never beat. The reading machine didn't go any faster than that.

High school is a strange time to begin with—going to high school in a church basement without accredited teachers took it to a whole new level. We managed to make it fun. We even had a volleyball team and a wrestling team.

We went to annual competitions with other Christian schools, where we competed in all kinds of areas, but our strength was music. We had a good choir. We frequently placed in the top three, sometimes winning first place. Our little choir traveled to other churches and performed concerts in matching home-sewn dresses for the girls, and matching suits and ties for the guys. We even recorded a cassette tape. My flute playing was featured on a couple of the songs.

One of the very few things I missed about public school was playing an instrument. I had enjoyed playing drums in the junior high band, but that didn't last very long because our band teacher was unacquainted with personal hygiene, making the music room a very unpleasant place to be. Someone started calling him Mr. Cardigan, because he was a real "sweater," and the name stuck.

I quit band and took a study hall that hour. It was boring, but at least it didn't nauseate me and leave me with a headache.

When I entered Christian school with no opportunity to play in a band, my parents told me I could choose an instrument and take lessons. I chose the flute, mostly because none of my siblings had played the flute. My sister-in-law, the one living down the road with the aforementioned adorable nephews and niece, agreed to teach me, since she played flute as well.

Playing the flute was one of my favorite things about that time. My sis-in-law was a good teacher, and I became decently accomplished. But again, I only had myself to compare to until another friend from school decided to take flute lessons from her, too. My friend and I played duets in church sometimes, and that was fun.

Shopping with Mom became more fun and less stressful. We would often head out after school together to the nearby larger town for groceries or fabric, among other things. It was comfortable and fun. Mom had less stress without so many kids at home. Finances had eased a bit with most of my siblings married and/or self-supporting.

Stopping to look at a pretty dress in a shop window used to be, "Don't even bother to look at that—you know we can't afford it," followed by her gripping my arm tightly and dragging me along to keep up with her. Now it was, "That's pretty—I wonder if we can put a couple patterns together and sew it?"

Sewing was a big bond for Mom and me. She taught me to sew when I was 12. I started begging her to teach me at age 10, only to be denied. She explained there was only one sewing machine and too many sisters learning. I had to wait my turn. Fair enough—I was good at waiting.

Turns out I was also good at sewing. I loved it. I always had a project on the go. Mom had the machine during the days she wasn't working at school. I had use of it in the evenings when I wasn't crocheting in front of the tv. Mom taught me how to crochet too.

She was a kind and patient domestic arts teacher. She made me a "busy bag" like hers—a craft bag to hold whatever I was crocheting at the time. My dad got a kick out of both of us dragging our busy bags along whenever we spent any length of time on the road. With my siblings' college concerts and recitals to attend, and other siblings having babies, we spent a good bit of time on the road.

I spent a lot of time cooking and baking. I never did learn how to make bread, but I did do my share of the weekly baking. I learned the basics of cooking from Mom. She was a good cook.

We used organic whole foods from our garden before it was a thing. Funny how I used to think we were poor because we ate vegetables out of the garden instead of buying them in cans at the store like my town friends' moms did. I was an idiot.

We didn't have a lot of money, but we ate really well. No one else I knew was having steak once a week or enjoyed an unlimited supply of whole milk and butter and cheese and ice cream. There were definite perks to being a dairy farm kid.

What I didn't understand was the cabinet full of pretty spice and herb bottles that were never used. One afternoon when I was about 14 years old, I opened those pretty bottles one by one and smelled them. A whole new world of flavor opened up to me.

The next time Mom made chili and stepped away from the stove to tend to the laundry, I snuck a taste. It seemed a little bland to me. I opened bottles and smelled herbs until a few of them appealed to me. I dumped them in, gave it a stir, and skedaddled out of the kitchen before I was caught.

At supper, Dad tasted the chili and loved it. Mom tasted the chili, narrowed her eyes, and raised one eyebrow toward me. "This tastes different than it did an hour ago."

"I was just helping," I replied.

This was a big risk for me. Helping without being asked hadn't ended well for me in the past. I was counting on my master plan having created a new, more relaxed comfort level with my parents. I held my breath.

"I have to admit it does taste better," she said with a smile. "Just don't go too crazy with the spices."

It worked! I made a deliberate change to the recipe and it was accepted! My plan was succeeding. I was forging a new relationship with my parents and they were embracing this new normal. I felt safe and confident.

I was building a new connection with Dad, too. I was the only kid left, so I did all the outdoor chores while Dad did the milking, except for mornings and Sundays. I offered to help with those chore times too, but he insisted that I focus on getting ready for school and on taking Sundays off. I experienced a lot of back pain during my teens due to scoliosis. Dad was careful to not overwork me and gave me time off heavy chores when I needed it.

I got pretty good at scooting around the farm on the dirt bike and was quite proficient in the use of the skid loader as well. One weekend a sibling was home from college and observed me using the skid loader to haul hay bales.

"What does she think she is doing messing around on that thing?!"

Mom defended me. She reminded them I was doing all the extra chores in the evenings that they used to do.

"She works as hard on this farm as you ever did."

My hard work was noticed and appreciated. Even though I didn't hear it often—and when I did hear it, it was usually second hand—it still went a long way toward healing my heart.

I was noticed and appreciated by others as well. My parents regularly invited friends and guest preachers for Sunday dinner. It didn't take long for me to be bored with the after-meal coffee and conversation. I began the practice of clearing the table, re-filling coffee cups, and starting the dishes on my own.

Mom said, "You don't have to do that on your own. I'll be in to help you shortly."

"You've worked hard enough," I replied. "Relax and visit with your friends. I can do the dishes."

My parents' friends noticed and commented, "Aren't you lucky to have such a good daughter."

My parents saw me through new eyes. Yes, it was all part of my master plan. And yes, I absolutely manipulated the situation to show myself in a positive light, but I don't think that's a bad thing.

I think it's completely normal and healthy for a child to desire their parents' approval.

Given the lack of that kind of expression for the first 14 years of my life, why wouldn't I take advantage of an opportunity to let my parents

---

I would swallow a Tylenol I didn't need and take my lie back to bed with me.

---

see me through a new and more positive lens? I honestly had the very best intentions—I was so happy to finally be able to help ease my mom's load and not make her mad in the process.

My depression was steadily getting worse, however. Suicide ideation was still an almost daily thought pattern.

When I was 16, I would often wake up in the night feeling hopeless. I would go to the medicine cabinet searching for pills to take. Any kind of combination that would knock me out. I just wanted to sleep and not wake up.

Of course, there was nothing stronger than Tylenol. Sometimes Mom would hear me. She would come out of her bedroom wondering if I was okay. I would say I was fine; I just had a headache. I would swallow a Tylenol I didn't need and take my lie back to bed with me.

One night I bypassed the medicine cabinet and sat on the back steps once again staring at my dad's shotguns. My arms were longer than they had been the first time I'd done this.

I could figure out a way to make it work now that I had grown. Where would I do it? It couldn't be anywhere in the house—Mom would be mad at the mess. I couldn't do it in the grove of trees behind the house. Once they noticed I wasn't around and looked for me, it would be really hard for emergency responders to drag my dead body out through the trees and the bushes. I thought about how angry Mom and Dad would be if I shot myself. It would create chaos and a lot of inconvenience.

There would be the cost of long-distance phone calls to the sibs, the cost of a funeral. They didn't have that kind of money. I wouldn't be around to help Dad with the chores. And now there were nieces and nephews who I loved deeply. I couldn't imagine leaving them behind. I would miss them too much. There wouldn't be anyone patient enough to take them on kitten hunts and read to them and play with them for hours at a time when they came to the farm.

My thoughts turned to catastrophic events.

Maybe while driving to school I could veer into the opposite lane and a truck would run into me and kill me. Then it wouldn't be my fault. They might still be mad that the car was totalled, but at least I wouldn't be there to experience their anger.

Maybe if I run outside at just the right time during a summer storm a tornado would come along and just pick me up and take me away. That would be perfect—no mess left to clean up. The downside was waiting for a tornado. The odds weren't great that one would show up at just the right time and place.

I lost my appetite. I lost weight. It scared my parents. They threatened to take me to the doctor if I didn't start eating. I couldn't let that happen. I somehow knew if the layers of my psyche started to peel back like an onion there would have been severe consequences. I started eating again.

I was constructing a façade of happiness and accomplishments to hide my pain, and it was becoming more difficult to maintain that façade as time went on.

9

My Favorite Uncle

THE SUMMER I WAS SEVENTEEN some of the older sibs gathered at the farm. It may have been to discuss the pending loss of the family farm and my parents' looming bankruptcy. I remember I was sick with a summer cold, and my nieces and nephews weren't there. I tried to join the sibs as they sat under the massive spruce trees in the front yard discussing things like mortgages and debt. The conversation was way over my head, and I obviously had nothing to contribute.

I just couldn't do it. I could not sit there any longer pretending I wasn't being ignored. I was in rough shape both physically and mentally. I did not have what it took to keep the mask in place. I went back inside the house. It was well over an hour before anyone thought to wonder where I was. Mom came looking for me and found me laying on the couch.

MOM: Why aren't you outside with your brothers and sisters?

ME: What's the point? I have nothing in common with them. I don't fit. I have never fit in this family. They never wanted me to begin with. Why would they care if I'm there for a discussion about buying a house and mortgage rates? The kids aren't here. There's no reason for me to be out there.

Mom was upset. This was the first time I had ever laid it out like that.

Mom: Of course you are part of the family!
Me: It doesn't feel that way. It's never felt that way.
Mom: Well, just stop feeling that way.

Hmmmm. Okay then.

Now was definitely not the time to tell her I didn't have a headache last night when I was scouring the medicine cabinet yet again for anything I could swallow to end this pointless existence. Mom simply offered the advice she had been giving to herself her whole life, but even she knew it didn't work that way.

Mom became kinder and more understanding. I struggled hard during my last school year. I often felt sick to my stomach. I could only handle two to three days of school at a time before I just couldn't get out of bed. Before long Wednesday became a regular sick day for me. I was ahead on my PACEs and getting good grades, so my parents allowed me those sick days. They were worried about me. They were afraid of me becoming even more sick and losing weight and stopping eating like I had when I was 16.

My parents saw me doing my best. They saw me excelling when I could and crashing when I couldn't. They gave me space and opportunity to practice self care before it was even a thing.

It was tradition for the female siblings in our family to clean my great-uncle Henry's trailer home once a week for $5. My great-uncle Henry was a WW2 Navy veteran. He was at Pearl Harbor the day it was bombed. He had pictures of the destroyer he served on. He had lots of stories to tell.

No one else in my family was interested in him or his stories. To them, he was just fat, shaky, old Uncle Henry. He had Parkinson's and walked with a cane that he would use to reach out and try to snag me as I went by.

His wife had left him shortly after he returned from WW2. What we now know as PTSD was then termed "he just couldn't get it together." He was a local cop until he reached retirement age. His favorite hymn was "Master the Tempest Is Raging." He requested it without fail whenever there was a favorite hymn time at church. No one else wanted to sing it, but the pianist and organist knew they had to practice it because Henry would request it.

When I was 14, it was my turn to clean for Uncle Henry. I would walk from the church to his trailer home after school on Wednesdays, clean his house, and then walk to my grandparents for supper and attend prayer meeting with them. Then I would return home with my parents after choir practice.

He was always watching cartoons when I arrived. After that was the daily rerun of *Big Valley*. He had a thing for Barbara Stanwyck.

I would dust around his pictures and ask him about his ship and serving in the war. His face would light up and he go on and on about the ship, his buddies, and the one or two stories tame enough for a young church girl's ear.

To be honest I can't remember a single story he told me. What I do remember was how happy he was to be asked. It made his whole week that I showed interest in him and his life. I felt sad that it was so easy to make him smile, and that he was so disrespected by the rest of my family. I claimed him as my favorite uncle just because of the derision shown to him by everyone else.

Uncle Henry's health was on the decline. My grandparents (he was brother to my grandfather) tried every way they knew to convince him it was time to go into the nursing home in town. He flatly refused. There was no budging him. Cleaning his house every week, I noticed concerning signs of his failing health.

Parkinson's stole his mobility. He stopped sleeping in his bed. His legs grew black as blood pooled from sitting in his chair all day and sleeping in it at night. I scolded him every week about this and made him put his feet up while I was there. He would put them back down every so often, I think just so I would scold him again. He would get this twinkle in his eyes as he shook his head and told me I was a bossy fishwife. I would laugh and say, "Don't make me come over there and put them up for you!"

I knew upon my high school graduation there would be $500 from Uncle Henry. This was his standard gift for each of us, to help with college registration. One day when I came to clean, he had a question for me.

"When you graduate this year, do you want the $500 that the rest of the kids got, or do you want a sewing machine?"

I was dumbfounded. It had never occurred to me that I would be given this choice. "Wow! I don't know. Let me think about it and I will tell you next week."

I told my parents, and they were just as surprised. After a great deal of thought I told Uncle Henry that I would rather have the sewing machine. A sewing machine would last longer than $500. I could someday use it to sew clothes for my children. He smiled and said, "Alright. A sewing machine it is." Mom and I started planning my new college wardrobe we would sew together after I graduated from high school.

Christmas arrived. We went to my grandparent's house for Christmas dinner. Uncle Henry was sitting in Grandpa's chair.

"Where is she? Where's Lisa?" I heard him bellow from the living room.

"I'm here, Uncle Henry."

He shook his cane at the Christmas tree.

"There's somethin' there with your name on it." My eyes grew wide in shock.

This was unusual—our family was so large and our income so small that we never received gifts from extended family. The most gifts anyone received was three, and two of them were usually handmade. A gift under our grandparents' Christmas tree was an unprecedented event. A hush fell over the room as I approached the tree and said, "Uncle Henry, what have you done?"

He chuckled and said, "Just look, girl!"

Under the tree, wrapped in layers of red cellophane and tied with a big red bow, was a sewing machine. It was exactly like Mom's. Tears sprang to my eyes. "Uncle Henry! This was supposed to be for graduation!"

"I figured you'd want to do some sewing to get ready for college."

"Thank you so much!" I hugged him and wiped my eyes.

"You're not done yet—there's something else upstairs for you," he said as he shook his cane at the stairs. Now he was really grinning, and my sisters were building up a healthy steam of mad. They had never been given this kind of special treatment.

I climbed the stairs on shaky legs, wondering what on earth it could be and how was I going to deal with five angry sisters. In the upstairs hallway stood a sewing table designed for my machine, again, exactly like Mom's. Now the tears really flowed. I ran downstairs and hugged him and said thank you and you shouldn't have done that and I will use it forever ...

Mom confessed to me later that my sisters were indeed angry, but she defended me. "You have no idea the kind of messes that girl has to clean up after him. He can't hold his bowels anymore. She earned that sewing machine and I don't want to hear another word about it."

I don't know what shocked me more—the fact that Mom defended me to my sisters or the fact that she told me about it.

It wasn't the first time my mom defended me. One of my sisters was home one weekend with her husband. When I was heading to bed, I said good night to my mom who was sitting in her corner crocheting, and I hugged my dad from behind, gave him a peck on the cheek, and said goodnight to him. You would think this was no big deal. Except we weren't a touchy-feely-huggy family. This was something I intended to change as part of my four-years-only-child plan. My strategy was working nicely.

My sister was horrified.

"I can't believe she just did that! That was so inappropriate!"

My mom stepped up. "How is it inappropriate for a daughter to kiss her father goodnight and tell him she loves him?"

Thanks, Mom. I needed and appreciated your backup.

I was counting the days until I would graduate and leave for college. Then my life could really begin. I could carve out a place in this world where I finally, completely, fully fit.

Just kidding—my eight siblings had paved the way before me to that very same tiny legalistic Baptist college. I was still just someone's little sister. They recognized me by genetic resemblance and musical talent, but it was several weeks before some of my professors could remember my first name. My music prof never once used my first name. He always called me by my last name, as if acknowledging my individual identity was too much of a bother. I expected nothing more.

10

College Girl

LATE AUGUST 1983. IT WAS hot and humid like only southern Minnesota can be. No air conditioning in the cinder block dormitories with small windows, and very little natural air flow.

I didn't care. I was so excited to finally be at college as a student. I met my new roommate—a senior who was a bit overwhelmed by my enthusiasm. I made her coffee in my little 2-cup coffee maker even when she insisted she didn't want any. I was practically bouncing off the walls in excitement to have my assigned mailbox, class schedule, and so many new boys to meet.

I was at college for my Mrs. degree, as we called it then. I wasn't interested in training for a career. I just wanted to get married and have babies. I signed up for elementary education, because it seemed like the best mom-job.

A Bible major was required, so I chose elementary education (El Ed) as my second major, and music as a minor.

That El Ed major didn't last long. Shortly into my sophomore year, one of my professors, after looking at my lesson plan assignment, looked at me in front of the entire class and said, "Please don't ever teach my son." I immediately dropped that major. And to be honest, since I was counting the days until I didn't have to go to school anymore, I had no business training for a career in education.

I found old friends and made new friends through the music program. I signed up for concert choir, symphonic wind ensemble, flute lessons, and voice lessons.

I had never played in a band, at least not since 7th grade when I was still in public school. Not to brag, but I was the best bass drum player they had in junior high band that year. Pretty decent on the snare as well. But I digress.

Oh, and there was that one summer I went to band camp. That was my first large band experience. I was playing flute by then. I wasn't too shabby, but I had never read band music before. That was a steep learning curve!

The only choirs I had ever sung in were the church kids' choir, the church choir, and the church school choir. They were all approximately 10 to 12 voices. Now I was in a concert choir of nearly 100.

I had never sat in a lecture style class before. I didn't know how to take notes. I didn't know how to use the library to do research for a paper. I didn't know what a paper was, let alone how to write one. I was way out of my depth academically. I had done well with my little high school workbooks, but I was completely unprepared for college courses.

My next eldest sister was completing her final year as I was starting my first year. We were next door neighbors in the dorm, which was very helpful to me. I owe her all the credit for my surviving that first year.

She helped me get a job at the fast-food place where she worked. She shared her car with me. I shared my clothes with her. She helped me settle into a new job, college life, dorm life, and dorm etiquette.

I would have quit symphonic wind ensemble if it wasn't for her. I was last chair flute. I was terrified. I was playing with kids that had been playing in orchestras for years. By the time we were preparing for the Christmas concert I went to her in tears. I couldn't do this. It was too hard. I felt like a fraud because I was faking more notes than I was playing.

She wouldn't let me quit. She kept encouraging me. Little by little, I was gaining confidence in my lessons. My flute professor was kind and understanding. He knew my family and where I came from and that this was all new to me. He pushed me to spend more time in the practice room, knowing it would pay off for me sooner than later.

When facing the giant of a term paper left me paralysed in fear, my sister took me to the library. She showed me how to find the reference books I needed, how to make an outline, and basically wrote the whole thing for me.

I needed no help socializing. Making friends came easily to me. I quickly found my tribe. We gathered at the same table in the dining hall for meals. We hung out in the coffee shop together. We formed study groups for exams.

Thanksgiving break arrived and my sister and I went to the farm for the long weekend. Just as we were packing the car to go back to campus, the phone call came to notify our family that our grandfather had passed away quietly at home in his sleep. Dad called the college to inform them that we would be staying home an extra week due to the funeral.

My parents had to drive to the airport in Minneapolis to pick up my aunt. They asked if I would stay with Grandma until they returned. Of course, I was happy to. I had a special relationship with my grandparents.

One of my aunts had played flute in high school, so Grandma loved to hear me practice on Wednesdays after I cleaned Uncle Henry's house. She used to say to me, "You go sing for your supper now. Supper will be ready in half an hour." I would go in the other room and practice my flute, leaving the door cracked open so she could hear me.

Supper was usually Swedish apple pancakes. Another Grandma-ism: "Eat until you are full and then one more to be sure."

Grandpa loved crossword puzzles. His favorite thing was to find some obscure word and use it in a sentence with me to see if I knew what it meant. Of course, I never did. That made him chuckle, and he would tell me the meaning.

These and so many more memories flooded my mind while I waited in Grandpa's chair for Mom and Dad to arrive with my aunt. Grandma ate a little at supper time and then went to bed.

When my parents and aunt arrived, my aunt went to wake Grandma, then my parents took me home. Mom commented that she was surprised to find me curled up in Grandpa's chair. I explained it felt comforting, like I was little again, curled up on his lap while he read to me. He was the only one who would read my favorite book to me over and over again without complaining. He smelled warm and cozy. And he always had a smile for me.

At the funeral Uncle Henry gestured for me to come over to him. He wanted me to sit with him in the service. Mom disapproved, feeling this was inappropriate because I should be sitting with immediate family rather than one row back with extended family. But Uncle Henry insisted so I supported him as he walked down the aisle with his cane to the pew and held his arm during the service. I rode with him to the cemetery and supported him as we stood by the grave. I sat with him during the reception, refilling his coffee and plate as needed.

I didn't mind in the least. It gave me a job to do. I wasn't left to wonder where to sit or who to sit by. Most of my nieces and nephews were there, so I hung out with them when Uncle Henry didn't need me anymore. Then it was back to school, catching up on class notes and missed assignments.

At my fast-food job, I was asked to work early mornings on the weekends making their breakfast biscuits. They had lost their weekend biscuit baker and hoped the poor college kid would be willing to pick up some extra shifts. What they didn't know was that I was a farm girl who had been baking for years. I knew how to not overwork the dough. The customer compliments poured in, and I became the weekend baker.

The only drawback was having to get up at 4 am to be at work by 5, then trying to catch a nap in my dorm room when all the chatty girls on my floor found it necessary to talk and laugh in the hallway outside my door. They didn't care when I asked them to please take it somewhere else, because I was trying to sleep after an early work shift. When my graduating senior sister came out in the hall to back me up, they took their little party elsewhere. Have I mentioned that I survived that first year only because of her?

Somehow, I managed to pass my classes and it was time to go home to the farm for the summer.

I made the most of spending time with my little nephews and baby niece. I used to take the boys into town for ice cream at the drive-in I had worked at during my high school summers. I took them to the park whenever I could. I had missed them a lot while I was away at school.

11

Falling In Love

WHEN I RETURNED TO COLLEGE for my sophomore year, I was on my own as my sister had graduated and moved to the city to work. I had a new roommate, and we became good friends. She was a trusted confidante. And she had a front row seat to the dramatic saga as I fell in love.

I was no newbie to campus life. I knew the best seats in the chapel for the first service of the year were front row center in the balcony. From there we could look down on the main doors and watch all the boys come in.

That one is dating. That one is a freshman, so, no. Already dated that one. That one is a jerk. Wait a minute ...

Who is that cute guy in the tan suit with the brown shirt and brown tie and brown hair?? My friends were quick on the uptake, and loyal to our sisterhood. They knew to back away from this guy. Bonus!! He's Canadian!!

The next day I discovered he was in my Psych 101 class. Right behind me. Thank God for alphabetical seating! As luck would have it the guy sitting next to me was his roommate. Well, wasn't that convenient!

Thanks to his roommate I learned his name. Next class as I went to my seat, I smiled at him and said, "Hi Steve." And the next class. And the next. He was shy. I was having fun watching him blush.

A few weeks went by, and I noticed him working on the custodial crew raking leaves. I'd smile and say hi and keep walking.

He had a buddy on the custodial crew, who came up to me one day and said, "If Steve asks you out, would you say yes?"

What was this—7th grade gym class? Check yes or no?

"Why isn't he the one asking me this?"

"He's shy, but he likes you. He just doesn't want to get shot down."

"I don't know ..."

"C'mon Lisa—he's a really nice guy but he needs someone to liven him

---

I had a three page paper due the next day that I hadn't started yet. Or I could go on a date.

up. And you are just the girl to break him out of his shell."

Oh. Good. Grief.

"Fine. Tell him that I'll go out with him, but he has to call me himself."

That year I was waitressing at a local steakhouse. The manager was a pig who hired me for my legs (his words), but it paid better than the fast-food joint, and I got to keep my tips. One night I was supposed to work until closing, but there were no customers. At all. Probably because of the crappy management, but at least I got to leave early. Just as I was walking onto the floor of my dorm, the phone rang.

Every floor had one phone in the hall entrance. It was tricky to find it available as its use wasn't limited to only that floor. If the phone on your floor was busy, you ran up or down to the other floors to see if their phone was free. So, it was kind of weird that the phone was available at 7:30 and it rang just as I walked in the door.

It was Steve. Would I like to go to the Dipper (the coffee shop on campus) for an ice cream?

Hmmm. I had a three-page paper due the next day that I hadn't started yet. Or I could go on a date. That was an easy call. "I'd love to! Give me 15 minutes to change out of my work uniform."

He was cute. He was charming. He asked questions about me and my family, so that kept me talking for an hour, but he didn't seem to mind. He admitted that he had borrowed someone's college yearbook from last year so he could learn my name. That's why it took him a few days to call me and ask me out.

He smiled at me. I made him laugh. He had the most beautiful Hershey-kiss-chocolate-brown eyes I had ever seen. Cue the tummy flutters!

There was only one catch. He had recently dated a friend of mine. I remembered commiserating with her when he broke up with her after only a few dates. What a jerk!

Girl-code mandated that I get her permission if this was to go any further. She was kind and understanding and by then had realized he wasn't the one for her. She had her eye on someone else. And so began my slide into true love.

He was welcomed by my friends at the "music people" table in the dining hall. He walked me to class and picked me up to walk me to supper when I wasn't at work. His roommate started dating my best friend.

His first visit to the family farm was the Thanksgiving weekend that one of my siblings got married. In my experience from watching my siblings bring home dates to meet the family, the best method to see if a new boyfriend had long term potential was to toss him in the deep end and see if he floated.

Everyone was home for the wedding with their families. Little kids everywhere. Steve had never been part of such a big family—he had only one brother and a few cousins. And he had never been around little kids or babies before. This was going to be interesting!

He made the rounds meeting everyone, with reassurance that there was no pressure to remember the 20 names he had just learned. My parents already liked him better than the other guys I had dated, but to be honest I hadn't set the bar very high in the past.

Steve was sitting in the middle of the couch, flanked by a sibling on either side, when my 2-year-old niece climbed up on his lap, dragging her blankie along with her. Steve's reaction was priceless! His eyes went big and he didn't know what to do with his arms. My niece snuggled in under his chin and looked over her shoulder at me with a look that said, *I'm stealing your boyfriend. What are you going to do about it?*

I busted out laughing, as did everyone else. From that moment on, she claimed him as a favorite uncle. My sister-in-law—mother of my boyfriend-stealing niece—said, "He's a keeper!"

This was not a statement made lightly—she had called the last three spouses to join our family "keepers." She had a knack for knowing which boyfriend or girlfriend would pass the test of time and our family. I warned her it was early days, way too soon to predict anything long term, but secretly I agreed with her. She just smiled and said, "Wait and see."

Obviously, I didn't tell Steve about this prediction, but word got around the rest of the family. He was being watched and I got plenty of sly side-eyes that weekend. And Steve spent a lot of time with my niece cuddled up on his lap.

I had a great boyfriend. I was a good server and asked by my new manager (who replaced the aforementioned pig) to train the new servers. I was in a traveling vocal ensemble for school. We traveled almost every weekend to churches, sometimes out of state, for the purposes of fundraising for the school and recruiting new students.

In February, I went with Steve to the Valentine Formal. It was the premier date night of the year. It was a beautiful evening. I borrowed a long red dress from a friend. We got our pictures taken and had a wonderful time with our friends. Steve bought me a corsage. The meal was delicious and the gym was decorated beautifully.

There was no dancing of course, because this was an independent fundamentalist Baptist Bible college. The six-inch rule separating dating couples was in effect, and there were actually people with rulers ready to measure if necessary. There were fun games to play, however, and we had a good time with our friends.

There is no way to ask for help if you don't know why you need it.

When Steve dropped me off at my dorm at the end of the night, I knew I should feel wonderful after a fun, romantic evening, but I was miserable. He could tell something was wrong and of course wondered what he had done to disappoint me. I tried to reassure him. He had been the perfect date. I did have a nice time. I didn't know why I was feeling this way. Maybe I'd feel better after a good sleep.

I didn't. I couldn't get out of bed. My roommate was worried about me. She tried to get me to go to breakfast with her, then lunch, but I just couldn't get up. She saw Steve at lunch and told him I wouldn't get out of bed. He was worried I hadn't eaten, so he went to McDonalds and got me a burger and fries. He sent it down to my room with a girl who happened to be walking into the dorm. I called him to say thank you, ate a bit, and went back to bed.

I did get up for supper, because Steve and my roommate would have freaked out if I hadn't.

I did what I did best—I sucked it up and pretended everything was fine. I said I just needed rest and now that I had gotten some sleep, I felt much better. In short, I lied through my teeth because they couldn't handle the truth, and I didn't know what to do about the truth. I was clinically depressed. I had been since my molestation. But since I had successfully trained my brain to forget about that, I was left with all the fallout and no way to understand it. There is no way to ask for help if you don't know why you need it.

12

Mono and the Big Breakup

OUR VOCAL ENSEMBLE WENT ON tour over spring break. I saw a great deal of the upper Midwest from the window of one of two campus vans. Steve spent spring break with my parents at the farm. He was worried that it would be weird without me there, but he had a great time. He studied and played Pac-Man. Mom fed him and did his laundry and sent him back to campus loaded down with all kinds of home baked goods.

I was becoming increasingly fatigued, creeping ever closer to complete exhaustion. I was carrying a full class load. I was in ensemble rehearsals, orchestra rehearsals, vocal lessons, flute lessons, and practice rooms, fulfilling the required practice hours for my music minor. I worked at the restaurant an average of 20 hours a week. I studied when I could. I got terrible grades, but I had lots of friends. The one thing I didn't do was sleep.

One day near the end of the school year I was in concert choir rehearsal. We were preparing for the commencement concert. Although I wasn't aware of it at the time, I fell asleep while standing up singing. I woke up again, still standing, still singing. The music prof called me into his office. I thought I must be in trouble, but I had no idea for what.

He had seen me fall asleep. He was concerned for my health and told me to go to the doctor. He recognized the signs of mono, as his daughter, who lived a few doors down from me in the dorm, was dealing with it that same semester.

I said I was fine, just tired, and promised to check myself into the campus infirmary for exhaustion, which I did. I slept a full 23 hours straight. Steve came to visit me, and I told him I felt like I had slept the day away. He said, "You're right. You slept an entire day away. Almost 24 hours."

I said, "That can't be right. I couldn't have slept that long—I'm still tired."

I didn't have time to go to the doctor. I had final exams. I had work. I had endless choir, orchestra, and vocal ensemble rehearsals. My plan was to stay in town for the summer, share an apartment with a couple friends, and work as many shifts at the restaurant as I could get. There would be time to go to the doctor when school was done.

I kept putting it off until I couldn't anymore. My throat swelled up, making me look like I had the mumps. My boss wouldn't let me work until I saw a doctor. I got swabbed and diagnosed with mononucleosis. I went home to the farm and slept for a month. Finally, after five weeks of sleeping, my blood test came back negative for mono, and I went back to my apartment to work the rest of the summer.

Being sidelined by mono was not the summer I had been expecting. While I was home sick my only contact with Steve was a few phone calls. He broke up with me. I honestly don't blame him. I would have dumped me too.

I was a mess. I was stuck in the deepest rut of depression I had ever experienced. I increasingly entertained thoughts of suicide. None of this was new—I had been in this unhealthy place for a long time. Steve had no point of reference for this, however. I was more than anyone could deal with. I had already lost friends over my depression. I was scared for my parents' financial future. They were facing retirement age with no ability to retire and no savings to fall back on. My dad was picking up construction jobs, driving school bus, anything to bring in some type of income. Mom's anxiety and depression returned with a vengeance. The best I could do for them was to leave home and not be one more mouth to feed.

This reinforced my belief that at the end of the day, as much as my parents may have loved me, I was only a liability. Another mouth to feed that they couldn't afford. Another car to maintain. Another doctor bill to pay if I got sick. No amount of my helpfulness and humor and charming their friends could make up for that.

During my sophomore year, I had gotten to know a girl who also came from a large Midwest farm family. We had a lot in common. I turned to her for support with my grief and fear of my parents losing the farm. She welcomed me into her room and listened to me. Twice. After that she avoided me like the plague. She was never in her room. She was too busy for a chat. She was unavailable in every sense of the word.

Near the end of the school year, my friend group went to a near by park to hike and hang out. I found out too late. I was not invited. I asked the question. I knew the answer, but I asked anyway.

"Why didn't you tell me you guys were going?"

"You're just not much fun to be around anymore."

Message received. Friendship ended.

So, when Steve broke up with me it wasn't much of a shock. I had been getting hints from many others for a while that I was dump-worthy.

I recovered from mono. I went back to college town, my shared apartment, and my job.

13

I Dated a Townie

I NEEDED EVERY SHIFT I could get to make up for lost time being sick. The steakhouse I worked at was part of a franchise chain, and there was another one in the next town over. I worked lunch shift there and dinner shift at home.

I was good friends with a girl who worked on the serving line at our restaurant. We made friends with a pair of brothers that worked in the same restaurant in the next town over. She and I often picked up extra lunch shifts there. We got invited to a demolition derby the brothers were driving in. Sounded like fun.

By the end of the night, I was riding on the tractor with the brother whose car got totalled, so he was towing it home. I'm a farm girl. I liked tractors. I liked cute guys. I had some revenge dating to do.

My friend and I double-dated the brothers all that summer. My big mistake was skipping church too often and being seen at the local county fair holding hands with said guy.

Summer was over. Fling was over. School started again. My junior year came with a significant downturn in enrollment. Significant enough that I got my own room, which was a huge bonus.

My junior year also came with unprecedented reprisals for me.

You see, there were very strict rules at the college about EVERYTHING. Especially dating. I was seen dating a "townie." Punishment must be meted out.

I was expelled from the traveling vocal ensemble because dating a townie called my character into question. I was no longer fit to represent the college.

Wow. Ok then. I tried walking the aisle at chapel to "get right with God." Nope. Not good enough.

It's not like I slept with the guy and got pregnant or started drinking and ran around town toting a bottle in a brown paper bag. The previous year, a guy snuck into the girl's dorm during spring break to see his girlfriend and got her pregnant. I only went to the county fair and held hands.

That guy who got his girlfriend pregnant wasn't in the spotlight, however, traveling around promoting the college. That was me. And *they were* both immediately expelled. At least I didn't get kicked out. This time.

Well, I thought, at least I'll get a little extra sleep on the weekends and pick up some extra shifts at work.

I did my time on the sidelines. Steve and I got back together. He decided if he didn't want to date me, but didn't want anyone else to date me, then maybe he wanted to date me.

Before you start thinking my guy was acting like a flake, I made him work for it. I also need to explain how dating at a cult college (aka fundamentalist college) works, or at least, how it worked back then.

But first: to the churchy folks that may be reading this, try to check your defensiveness and resist the overwhelming urge to send me your livid emails condemning me over calling my college a cult. Let's revisit our sense of humor here.

Because most of it was really funny!!

14

Fun Facts about Cult College

FUN FACTS ABOUT CULT COLLEGE:

- Dating is highly structured and closely monitored.
- Dating couples could go to The Dipper, which was a small coffee and snack shop on campus, with wide open sight lines, closely monitored for inappropriate behavior.
- They could go to the gym for a basketball game, or to the athletic field for football or soccer. Our sports teams rarely won any of their games, so not much to see there.
- They could eat meals together in the dining hall. They could walk around campus. They could linger on the provided benches lining the sidewalks and have a conversation, in full view under bright lights after dark.
- A couple could even go to the game room for video games or billiards.
- There were perception rules, however. These were unwritten, yet written in stone.

- If a guy walked you to class, you might be dating.
- If he took you to supper in the dining hall three times, you were absolutely dating.
- If a guy took you for a slow stroll around campus and you stopped to sit on one of the brightly lit benches, there was a ring in your future.

So, to be fair, I totally get why Steve was nervous about getting back together. That was a whole new level of dating that usually involved a promise ring. Mine has a beautiful pearl in a delicately swirled gold setting.

There was one more place on campus to have a date, which was frequented by only the most committed couples. The Dating Parlor.

Yes, you read correctly. Dating. Parlor.

This was a large lobby area on the ground floor of the girls' dorm. There were two tiers. It was furnished with generous-sized love seats, and a table or two with chairs, should a couple need to spread out the books and study for an exam.

There was also a desk staffed by the Dating Monitor. The good ones kept their heads down and studied until the Dating Parlor closed at 9:55, so the guys could be back in their own dorm by 10:00 curfew.

The annoying ones kept their heads up and their eyes narrowed, diligently scoping out the room for inappropriate behavior. They periodically tapped the 6-inch ruler on their desk, reminding the couples that at any time the ruler may be brought forth, and there better be at least 6 inches of space between the young lovers or they would be evicted. And yes, that actually happened. I was there when a couple got measured, more than once. Different couples.

The snack of choice in the Dating Parlor was microwave popcorn. There was a microwave in the second-floor lounge. The girlfriends would line up to nuke their bag of popcorn to share with their stud muffins. And if they accidentally reached for a handful out of the bag at the same time ... ? The betting pools swung into action over when the ring would appear on her hand.

I am aware that my voice is overly sarcastic, and I am shamelessly pandering for the easy laugh. But SERIOUSLY!!! How is this not hilarious?!

By the way, no one called it the Dating Parlor. We called it the Passion Pit, also sarcastically, because no passion was happening in that pit.

There was also a highly structured discipline system called DEMERITS.

Each student was allotted 150 demerits per semester. Fifty demerits got you a warning. One hundred demerits got you confined to campus, except for going to a job or going to church. Hitting the big 150 got you expelled, or "shipped."

Examples of demerit-worthy behavior included, but were not limited to:

- Being late for class
- Skipping class
- Not emptying your trash daily
- Not tidying your room daily
- Leaving campus without a signed permission slip
- Not signing out when leaving campus
- Not signing in when returning to campus
- Dating infractions

Dating off campus without a signed permission slip, not signing out for said date, not signing in after said date, and not bringing along an approved chaperone? You might as well pack your bags and quit school before you get shipped.

When I brought my boyfriend home to the farm for the weekend, we selected our chaperones very carefully. The two of us going home for the weekend meant three people going to the farm for the weekend. When we went with another couple, we were allowed to "double date" without a fifth person as a chaperone, on the honor system that we would keep each other accountable in a mutually-assured-destruction kind of way. Everyone loved my parents, so we had to beat chaperones off with a stick.

I got demerits for leaving my high school jacket displayed on the back of my desk chair. Apparently, the floor supervisor inspecting the rooms during chapel that day decided it belonged in the closet, not proudly displayed for all to see.

And yes, there was daily required chapel, during which you better have bribed your chapel row monitor so they didn't report you missing, and you had better have found a hiding place other than your room if you wanted to skip chapel.

My friends and I willingly complied with the demerit system, but we didn't call them demerits. We called them Units Of Fun. They were to be carefully budgeted, because you didn't want to spend them on stupid stuff like a tissue in your trash or a late library book. And they *absolutely* were going to be spent, so the cost had better be worth it.

This is what happens when you send the youngest of nine to the same Bible college all her siblings had attended before her—the youngest watches and learns. I was diligent in my continual observations and analyzing the results of the choices of my older siblings. My analysis didn't discourage me from infractions. I simply learned how not to get caught.

All sarcasm and joking aside, I loved my years at Bible college. There was a lot to be frustrated by, to be sure, but I had a blast.

15

DVBS Tour

ASIDE FROM MY SOUL-CRUSHING BOUTS of depression, when I could only wish I was back on the farm with access to my dad's guns, I had wonderful friends who stood by me when the chips were down. I had an amazing boyfriend who became my amazing husband. I learned a lot about people traveling around the Midwest with music groups. Thanks to a certain housewife in Wisconsin, I have a killer potato recipe!

I learned how to stick with something even when it was hard and overwhelming, and my grades sucked because I didn't know what I was doing, or I just didn't care and went out on dates instead of writing papers. I learned how to get along with people at work, who thought my college was a cult. I mean, they kind of weren't wrong ...

I learned I wasn't stupid after all. I was at least smart enough to receive a BSc in Bible, with added Music (Applied Flute) and English minors. Not to brag, but Steve and I were also named to the Who's Who of American Colleges and Universities for 1987. I guarantee it wasn't because of my grades.

In the spring of the school year, select students were assigned to traveling music groups who toured the US during the summer, fundraising and recruiting potential students. Because of my rebellious behavior the summer before my junior year, I was not worthy of such an honor.

But I was worthy of a brand-new kind of summer tour. Daily Vacation Bible School tour.

I was selected to be one of a team of three, traveling to churches to run their DVBS program. We were mentored by the most favorite prof on campus. We selected a curriculum. We prepared our materials. We sent prep packages to the churches so they could prepare props and set designs in anticipation of our arrival.

I don't remember the name of the theme. It had something to do with desert safari. The guy in our group wore khakis and a pith helmet and did all the emcee stuff. He was a good guy. Kind and patient. The other girl was very nice as well, daughter of a professor. She handled the Bible memory contest and did some teaching.

I was the puppet master and the storyteller. During a weekend visit to my parent's farm, I sewed two hand puppets. One was a dark gray scraggly looking rat named Dirk the Desert Rat. The other was a friendly looking camel named Omar. I developed distinct voices for them. I also made a mummy costume out of old sweatpants and a sweatshirt and a ripped up old sheet from my mom's linen closet.

Each church would prepare a puppet hut for me to use—always on stage in front of a door so I could access it without being seen.

During the opening session of Day One the puppets would appear, welcoming the kids and getting the day off to a fun start. This was followed by Bible teaching, Bible verse memorization, Kool-Aid and cookies, and a missionary story (that was me). Closing session brought the puppets back, and at some point, someone, usually the pastor, would stick his arm into the sleeve of the mummy and wave it around in the baptism tank. Kids would see the mummy arm sticking out and go wild. The leader guy would pretend not to see it and the kids would go even more wild.

Day Two, closing session, the kids would see an arm and part of the head. More mayhem ensued.

And so on and so on until the last day, when the mummy ran around the sanctuary, chased by leader guy. Around and over the pews, the kids screaming and cheering him on. How crazy the chase got was determined by how athletic the mummy was. Most of the time the pastor handed it off to a teenager by the last day. Basically, whoever fit in the suit got the gig.

It was the best summer break experience of my college career. Our little band of three saw a lot of the US Midwest. We were treated to a trip to the top of the Rocky Mountains outside Missoula, Montana. We were treated to dinner at The Old Spaghetti Factory in Kansas City. We were billeted in people's homes, where I learned to play boggle and collected another recipe, this one for monkey bread. It's still a family favorite.

But before I trotted around the country with my two DVBS cohorts, Steve took me home to New Brunswick, Canada to meet his family.

That was my first plane trip. We practically had the whole plane to ourselves. It was one of those 80s discount airlines. Does anyone remember People Express? You carried your own bags and brought your own food. And there were, like, five passengers on the entire flight. No wonder that airline was only around for a few years.

Steve's mom and her cousin picked us up from the airport in Bangor, Maine. She zipped around those twisty coastal roads like a Nascar pro. She got pulled over for speeding near the border. It could have been that processing a speeding ticket for a Canadian was too much paperwork, or it could have been her convincing story, but she talked her way out of the ticket.

Steve had one brother, still in high school and dating his high school sweetheart, so I didn't see much of him. Steve and his dad went to work together every morning to the nuclear power plant. I was in the house with his mother all day. I was so nervous! I was in love with this guy, and I really wanted his family to like me.

The first morning of my visit, I woke with an urgent need for the bathroom. I opened the door of my bedroom to see if the bathroom was open. Nope.

I tried again in a couple minutes—still no. At this point I was wondering if I was going to be able to hold it any longer. As I opened my door to check again, there was a crash and a cry of pain from Steve's brother's room next door.

Steve's dad opened his door across the hall at the same moment as I did. The poor man was in a state of shock, standing frozen in his doorway at the sight of me in my doorway, covered nose-to-toes in a white seersucker-with-pink-roses Laura Ashley-style nightgown (and matching robe!), complete with ruffles. I had made it myself.

I was equally frozen, shocked by the sight of my hopefully future father-in-law, wearing black speedo style underwear with white lacing up the front. Both doors slammed shut again!

Steve's brother had been lifting weights and dropped a barbell on his foot. Steve's dad heard the crash and yelp, and ran to respond without stopping for his robe. It took a few years for he and I to make eye contact without feeling embarrassed all over again!

I was terrified the first few days, so I didn't say much. I didn't know what to say or how to start a conversation with Steve's mom. I spent way too much time in the bathroom perfecting my makeup, trying to bolster my courage. As a result, Steve's family's first impression was not a good one. I appeared to be overly concerned with my looks, with an arrogant, holier-than-thou religious vibe.

To be fair, they were not fans of Steve going to Bible college to begin with. They would have preferred that he stay home, get his electrical engineering degree, and marry a nice Maritime girl who would give them nice Maritime grandbabies. They had been counting on him doing one year at Bible college, getting it out of his system, and coming back home.

They did not count on him meeting a Midwestern farm girl, marrying said girl, and staying west for 20 years. As a result, before they even met me, they were not a fan of me for taking their son away from them.

I spent most of my time that first visit staring out the wall of windows looking out on the Bay of Fundy. This land-locked farm girl never tired of watching the tide roll out and roll back in.

I borrowed Steve's mom's sewing machine so I could finish a dress I was making for DVBS tour. I mended a couple loose buttons on Steve's dad's shirts. Mostly I was terrified I was making a bad impression on his family (which I was), and I dreaded having to say goodbye to Steve at the end of the week.

One family member welcomed me with open arms and with delight. Nanny was Steve's maternal grandmother. She had a mischievous bent that reminded me of my own grandmother. And she was delighted that Steve was attending a Bible college. She was the only one who supported that decision. Our oldest daughter carries her name as a middle name. I still miss Nanny.

She let me help in the kitchen, peppering me with questions about my family while we washed dishes. She gave me a big hug goodbye at the end of the evening. She told me she was so happy Steve had found a nice Christian girl. I was unsure of how Steve's parents felt about me, but I had done the best I could and hoped they would come to accept me in time.

I left with a kiss goodbye and the promise that Steve would write. I had given him my itinerary with all the addresses so he knew where I would be from one week to the next.

As we traveled and taught Bible verses and chased the mummy, I wrote letters. The guy on our team was getting letters from his girlfriend. The other girl was getting letters from her mom. By the time we were headed to our third church, I had not yet received any letters from Steve.

I created scenarios in my mind to explain this, each one crazier than the last. While the other girl slept in the back seat, the guy and I performed a complete autopsy on my visit to his parents. I must have done something terribly wrong, and they convinced him he should break up with me again. They remembered my desperate phone calls to him last year when he broke up with me.

The guy told me I was ridiculous. Steve still loved me. He was mailing the letters from Canada, so they were bound to be held up by international mail. The letters would catch up to me.

He was right. When we got to the next church, the pastor greeted us with a handful of mail. Three of those letters were mine, from Steve. My world was righted on its axis once again. I wept happy tears as I read each one over and over again. Steve was The One.

Somewhere in the middle of our summer tour we ended up back on campus for an overnight pit stop. The other girl stayed with her parents who lived in town. The guy and I looked at each other and grinned. No teachers. No dorm monitors. Just one sleepy security guard to avoid. We planned our evening—an exploration of the secret tunnels we knew existed but had never seen.

We met after dark in the place where he knew there was an access door. He went first with the flashlight. The tunnels were cramped, dark, and full of spider webs. We were Indiana Jones searching for the Holy Grail—the tunnel into the oldest campus building, which housed the bell tower.

Several years ago it had been used as auxiliary dorm space for the guys. Now it was home to the costume room for school plays, and prop/set storage. And there was The Door to the Bell Tower!

I know—it really wasn't that big of a deal. But it kinda was at the time. We were committing multiple infractions that would have used up most, if not all, of a semester's worth of Units Of Fun. And we were getting away with it!! We made a pact to never speak of it again. Which of course we broke, but only to highly trusted rule-breaking friends, who would, if they squealed on us, also face reprisals, because we had good dirt on them.

When summer tour ended I had two weeks back on the farm with my parents before I had to go back to school. Steve was flying back a week early to spend time with me. My parents went to the Minneapolis airport to pick him up. I don't remember why I didn't go along—I may still have been driving home from campus after the end of DVBS tour.

When I saw Steve again, the tummy flutters were bigger than ever, and my happy heart danced around in my chest.

I helped him take his bags up to his room. He took out a jeweler's box, opened it up, got down on one knee, and proposed. WAHOO!!!!!

We went downstairs and announced our engagement to my parents. They were thrilled. Mom examined the ring and got quite nervous when I tried on the matching wedding band. "Take that thing off—you're not married yet!"

We set the date, deciding on the day after Steve's grad to make it easier for his family to attend both his graduation and his wedding.

Mom went to the desk and pulled out a big notebook. She plopped it down in front of me and said, "Here you go. All the wedding plans from your sister's weddings."

Dad got up from his recliner, looked at Steve, and cleared his throat.

"There's a cow I need to check on in the barn. Steve, why don't you come with me."

I hadn't seen either of them move that fast in a very long time.

"You're both cowards!" I yelled at their scurrying backsides. And Mom and I began the first of many disagreements over my wedding. I had strong opinions about my wedding, and above all, I was determined that my wedding would be different from my sisters' weddings before mine.

I learned later that Steve and my parents' drive home from the airport had not been without notable moments. They stopped halfway at the Country Kitchen restaurant for a meal. Mom used the ladies' room. While she was away from the table, Steve asked Dad for permission to marry me. Mom came back to the table not privy to their conversation. She complained about the running toilet in the ladies' room. Dad said, "I can fix that," entered the ladies' bathroom, and fixed it. No unsuspecting female diners were scarred for life during that incident, except possibly my mother, and the one lady who walked into the bathroom and shrieked to find a man fiddling with the toilet. The manager was very grateful and offered them all a slice of pie on the house.

16

Wedding Plans and Campus Conflict

MY SENIOR YEAR AT COLLEGE was quite memorable for many reasons.

I returned to campus with an engagement ring on my finger. I wrote a number on each page of my day planner counting down to my wedding day. I was president of my society (that's Baptist Bible college speak for "sorority"). I was on the student council. I was preparing for my flute recital.

There were a lot of changes on campus as well, most notably in the athletic program. The college was in financial crisis.

We had been losing financial support from previously participating churches across the country. They were no longer sending their students to our college, recommending them to other colleges instead. The dorms were empty to the point that the entire fourth floor was completely vacant. Upperclassmen like me were guaranteed our own room, and only freshmen were required to have a roommate. There were a lot of empty rooms, even on the floors where students lived.

The big plan to reverse this trend was to invest in a winning football team, hopefully resulting in the churches who had passed us by resuming financial support and sending their students to us again.

The football team initiative had already started the year before. I remember going to the airport with a friend, at the request of the new coach to pick up a football player who had been recruited. When we arrived at the campus and passed by the big brick signage proclaiming this to be a Baptist Bible college, the guy was shocked. "Wait a minute! This is a Bible college?"

"Um, yes," I replied. "How did you not know that? Didn't they tell you when you were recruited?"

"NO! They told me I would be playing football in a better division than last year."

Now it was my turn to be shocked. Every student was there expressly because it was a Baptist Bible college. What was going on?

This was the second year of revamping the football program. There were more recruited players than ever. It seemed like there were as many non-Christian guys as Christian guys on the team—or more. This would have been fine if they had actually wanted to be there, go to class, and follow the rules. Most of the time, they didn't.

My friends and I struggled to understand how these guys got caught with beer in the dorm yet did not get disciplined. Anyone else would have been "campused" at the very least (not allowed to leave campus), if not expelled.

It was common knowledge that the coach had parties at his house for the football recruits and their girlfriends. This would not have been tolerated from any other professor or coach. And I can guarantee there wasn't a 6-inch ruler in sight.

However, somewhat magically, at the end of the football season all those infractions caught up with them and they were suddenly gone. I had questions, and the answers made no sense whatsoever.

I went to my dad with my questions. I told him everything. Then he had questions. And he wasn't going to stop until he had answers that did make sense.

My dad served on the board of trustees at my college, as he had for several years. He was well known to the faculty and staff for his integrity, and well known to the students for his hospitality at the farm when we brought friends home. When he was on campus for meetings, he didn't take his meals with the other board members. He sat with Steve and me and our friends. He wanted to know what the students were thinking and what they were concerned about.

Dad recommended that we start documenting the discrepancies and infractions we witnessed. I wasn't the only kid on campus who had the ear of a board member. Dad made sure the contact information of key board members found their way into the hands of key students. He told us to keep an accurate account of our concerns and write to the board members. I didn't write any letters—I just called home. Regularly.

In the meantime, campus life continued as usual. As members of the student council (Steve was the president), Steve and I helped plan social events. We had a fun country-style carnival in the gym, complete with hay bales and games and apple cider. We also organized a campus-wide Easter Egg Hunt.

The societies we belonged to were brother/sister societies, so we planned an outing to the local roller-skating rink. We rented out the entire place for a few hours one afternoon.

We brought our own college-approved music. Everyone was having a great time. And then the DJ played the Hokey Pokey.

We all made a big circle on the floor and did the Hokey Pokey on our roller skates. It was so fun!

Until chapel the next day, when the elderly Dean of Students got up and blasted us in front of everyone for dancing. We did our best to not laugh out loud, but it got pretty difficult when he began to wave his arms around and lectured us about "gyrating from side to side," delivered in his distinctive southern drawl. Later we laughed until we cried over the ridiculousness of this "inappropriate behavior," especially considering what the football players and their girlfriends were getting away with.

Second semester I took aerobics for my PE elective. Just a few weeks into the class our instructor told us she was pregnant again. As her pregnancy was considered high-risk, her doctor wouldn't allow her to teach aerobics anymore.

I sometimes laid in my bed feeling so hopeless, thinking about suicide, and feeling so confused about why I felt that way when I had so much to be happy about and look forward to.

She asked me to sub for her, which I was happy to do. I expected, at the very least, if I was subbing for an entire semester, I would get a credit on my school bill. I learned to never assume. I wasn't paid so much as a dime, and there was no credit on my school bill. She got paid for an entire semester for a class I taught. Oh well. At least I was staying in shape so I would fit into my wedding dress.

This was the same teacher who told me to never teach her son, yet subsequently hired me to babysit said son two mornings a week. I take pride in the fact that I was the first person to ever take him to the park down the street. I swear that stroller was only ever used when I was babysitting. I also kept up a steady stream of sage advice that likely fell on deaf ears at his tender age of one. Oh well. I tried.

One evening near the end of our aerobics class in the athletics building, a couple guys who had been using the pool in the basement popped their heads in. Just for fun, they jumped into the last few minutes of the class. Their antics and crazy aerobics moves had us all falling over laughing! Well, almost all of us.

One girl in the class did not find it funny. She reported me for letting guys come into a girls-only exercise class. I got reprimanded, but continued teaching the class. From then on, I was very careful not to have too much fun just in case she reported me again.

The endless cycle of school, work, dating, wedding planning, exhaustion, and depression continued. I sometimes laid in my bed feeling so hopeless, thinking about suicide, and feeling so confused about why I felt that way when I had so much to be happy about and look forward to. I was grateful to have a room to myself. I didn't have to keep it together for a roommate. But I did have to take a deep breath and practice my smile before I left my room to go out on campus. I needed someone who understood me and could explain myself to me. That was about as possible as hiding a pet unicorn in my dorm room.

Some of the football recruits came back for second semester, even though the football season was over, presumably to be with their girlfriends. I could only assume this to be true because they did only the bare minimum to get by.

My friends and I were becoming increasingly concerned about our school. We were comparing notes, writing to the board members, and having prayer meetings in our rooms.

One of my close friends, whom I regularly met for coffee between classes, was warned about being seen with me. Apparently I was labelled a troublemaker by the administration. My friend was told it would be in their best interest not to be seen with me.

Another friend had a parent working in the accounting department. This person had been compiling a secret file over time that proved disturbing financial discrepancies. This friend and her parent were talking on the phone one night after hours. The next day, she was approached by an administration member who repeated part of the private phone conversation from the night before and warned her to be very careful "who she associated with and who she talked to."

This was a new development. Another friend of mine had worked summers as a telephone operator, back when being a telephone operator was actually a job. She could tell by listening if a phone was tapped. There was a very specific clicking that you wouldn't notice unless you knew what to listen for.

My phone operator friend came to my room after hours. I called home to talk to my dad, with both of us listening on the earpiece. I shared my suspicions of phone tapping with my dad and while we were talking, we could hear a strange intermittent clicking. My friend nodded, confirming that my phone was being tapped at the switchboard in the administration office building. My dad could hear it too. Steve was working night watch on campus. He was keeping an eye on the switchboard room and saw the lights on when no one should have been there. When he checked it there were obvious signs that some one had just fled the room, leaving the door open and the light on. My dad told us if we needed to talk to him or any other board member we should use an off-campus phone, or the one on the unoccupied fourth floor of the dorm so there would be less chance of our call being monitored.

17

Calling Out Corruption

THE SITUATION ON CAMPUS WAS escalating. I was obviously being targeted. The administration was trying to scare me by scaring my friends. Clearly, they hadn't met me. Or they simply underestimated me and how much of my father I carried in my spirit.

One morning the president of the college pre-empted the chapel sermon. He spoke instead, talking about secret groups gathering in dorm rooms for the purpose of undermining the administration and harming the school. He said he'd had enough of the gossip running rampant in the dorms about faculty members and the administration. He offered to meet with any student at any time in his office. His office had an open door to anyone with concerns. We should go directly to him instead of indulging in the sinful practice of making false accusations in private.

One friend in particular had my back. She was a senior, set to graduate with honors in just a few months. She would sit quietly, bearing witness to my meeting with the president. She understood the risks. She had vowed that if they tried to kick me out, she would walk out with me. She was prepared to sacrifice a four-year music degree because she, too, believed that fighting corruption was a fight worth having.

We looked at each other, cut our next class, and went to his office. My dad had warned me to look for just this kind of opportunity. He also told me to not meet the president alone in his office unless I had a tape recorder to record the conversation. There had been so many discrepancies and outright lies that the administration couldn't be trusted. Our president was also a skilled gas-lighter.

My friend and I got past the secretary's disapproving glare, cassette recorder in hand, and the president welcomed us into his office.

I explained that I was responding to his invitation to bring my concerns directly to him, as he had stated in chapel just a few minutes ago. He wanted to know why my friend was there. I told him I was acting on the advice of my father, to either record our conversation on her tape recorder, or have her sit in as a witness. Mr. President was not amused, but he couldn't get away with booting my friend out of his office after he had offered an open invitation to the entire student body. He made it clear we were not allowed to record the conversation, however, which we expected.

What were my concerns and how could he help me with them?

- Football recruits that had no idea they were coming to a Bible college, then given a free pass to break all the rules if they won football games.
- Being told to shut up and just obey when I had questions for my teachers. (I was specifically told to "shut up and obey" by the head of the music department.)
- My friends being threatened because they spent time with me.
- My phone and my friends' phones being tapped and private conversations with parents used against us to manipulate us into submission.

82

- ♦ Disturbing financial discrepancies being covered up.

In short, this college that all nine of us siblings had attended, and that we looked forward to the next generation attending as well, was steeped in corruption and I could no longer, in good conscience, recommend this school to my nieces and nephews, or anyone else for that matter.

Oh—and we weren't gossiping in the dorms. We were on our faces before God pleading with Him to save our school.

His smile went from condescending to strained to an outright sneer. He asked me what I thought the root of all these problems was. I looked him steadily in the eye and said, "The root of all these problems lies with the administration."

All color left his face. He was visibly shaking, whether in anger or fear, I don't know. Probably a bit of both. Veins were popping out on his forehead.

"Young lady, do you understand what you are saying to me?!"

"Yes sir, I do, and it breaks my heart. Thank you for your time." And we left him sitting in his office, fuming. We knew there would be a price to pay, but we had poked the bear anyway.

The rest of that day passed in a bit of a blur.

I called my dad in the hospital (he had fallen from a high beam in a barn, where he was working as a construction supervisor, and broken his pelvis, resulting in a long hospital stay). I told him about my meeting with the president. He was proud of me for standing up for what was right. He was also prepared to deal with whatever consequences I might face,

The Dean of Women called me to her office off the lobby of our dorm. I had always liked her. Her daughter had been a friend of mine. That day she was angry with me. She asked, "What makes you think you can march into the president's office and tell him he's going to be fired?!"

I was dumbfounded. I tried to tell her that wasn't at all what was said. In fact, I had a witness to the conversation that could corroborate that I had said nothing of the kind. But she was having none of it. I was in big trouble, she said, and she suggested that I better watch it because I was in danger of being expelled.

I don't remember why I had to go to the admin building that afternoon—probably to go to the bookstore or make a payment on my school bill. I was approached in the hallway by the Dean of Admissions. He told me I had no business talking to my dad about the college and I better keep my opinions to myself or I would be expelled for disloyalty.

I called my dad's hospital room for the second time that day. He was livid. He assured me they had no authority to expel me.

I had let the genie out of the bottle and there was no putting it back now.

My friend who had witnessed the meeting and another mutual friend came to my room when I told them I was going to be expelled because I told the president my dad was coming to fire him. They were both graduating in a few weeks. They told me if I got shipped, they were leaving with me. They were both prepared to risk losing their degrees over this. The corruption had gone too far.

Steve called me. The Vice President of the college had pulled him aside and told him he better get me "under control" before we both got expelled for disloyalty. That one still makes me laugh!

My dad called back—conversation number three that day. Unprecedented. He told me I could expect a personal apology from the Dean of Admissions within 24 hours, and if it didn't happen to let him know. I got the apology.

The dean kept his job.

I had let the genie out of the bottle and there was no putting it back now. The letters from students to board members continued. My dad got out of the hospital. Key board members were in regular communication. An emergency board meeting was scheduled. The campus was buzzing with speculation. I kept my head down and went about my normal routine. When asked, I had no comment. The prayer meetings in the dorm continued. There was no way anyone was going to tell a bunch of Bible college kids they couldn't pray together.

In early spring the board came to the campus for their emergency meeting. They had spent the previous weeks gathering evidence, and boy did they ever uncover a mess. I don't know any further details about the evidence, but it was serious enough that several people got fired, starting with the president and the football coach.

The day of the meeting, I was walking from my dorm to the dining hall for lunch. The board had been behind closed doors all morning. I worried about my dad and how the meetings were going.

I looked up and saw, coming toward me on the sidewalk, fresh from the boardroom, none other than the football coach. There was nowhere to hide. My mind was yelling, *No! Don't come this way!*

So of course, he came my way. And he stopped me.

"So, I got fired," he stated. I braced myself for a verbal attack. "But I expected it," he continued. "I want you to know I really respect your father. He was the only one who had the guts to stand up, look me in the eye, tell me my behavior was wrong, and fire me. He has more integrity in his little finger than all rest of those theologians put together."

He walked away. I struggled to start breathing again. I knew my dad would act with courage and integrity even in the face of fear and opposition.

I was so proud of him. In that moment I determined to follow in his footsteps of integrity. No matter what.

I was even prouder of him considering that only he and one other member of the board of trustees did not have a doctorate in theology nor were they respected pastors of prominent churches. Yet my dad, the farmer, was the only one to literally stand up in that meeting and demand they do the right thing by cleaning house of the corruption that had been festering there for way too long. My dad didn't like to fight. But when it mattered, he could scorch the earth if he needed to.

An interim president was named and the announcement was made to the student body. The interim president held a town hall meeting, inviting the entire student body to come and air their grievances and concerns. The campus felt like a fresh wind had blown through, blowing away all the tension and worry.

I did not get expelled for disloyalty. In fact, I showed more loyalty than most by calling out the corruption when I saw it. We all finished the year strong, my friends got their diplomas, and Steve and I looked forward to our wedding.

18

The Wedding

THE DAY BEFORE GRADUATION, STEVE and I were given a special pass to drive to the airport, unchaperoned, to pick up his family. That was the day both our names were announced back-to-back to receive the award for being named to Who's Who in American Colleges and Universities. When neither of us went up to accept our awards, the whole student body responded with raised eyebrows and an "OOOOOO!" It was a small student body. Everyone knew we were getting married the next day.

At the airport, we met Steve's parents, Nanny, his brother, and his aunt and uncle. His brother and uncle were both groomsmen. And the whirlwind wedding weekend began.

Steve's family rented two white Lincoln Towne cars. They were meant to follow us back to campus and their hotel. They weren't used to roads bigger than the occasional four lane stretch of highway. The Minneapolis highway interchanges, that looked more like spaghetti junctions, were a bit of a challenge for them to say the least. As Steve drove, I kept an eye on the cars behind us to be sure they were still there. At one point they weren't able to make a lane change and, as we continued down the highway, we saw out our side windows two white Lincoln Towne cars on the wrong exit ramp.

We pulled over and tried not to panic. Before long they found their way back and pulled over behind us. Steve promised to do a better job leading. His dad and uncle promised to a better job following, and we made it back to campus with no further incident.

Steve's brother spent the night on campus, getting the full tour and meeting all Steve's friends. I finished packing up my dorm room for the last time. Steve and I had found a tiny one bedroom converted apartment on the second floor of an old character home. We had spent that last week on campus packing and moving our belongings into our new apartment.

After commencement we moved the last load, packed the cars, and headed to the farm. We dropped his family at the nearest motel, which wasn't exactly nearby. There were no accommodations in our tiny town. They had to go 30 miles to find a town big enough to have a motel.

Steve, who was staying with them overnight, got them checked in and made sure they had the maps required to navigate the back roads of southwestern Minnesota. I headed to the church in my parents' town, in the opposite direction, to set up and get ready for the rehearsal and the rehearsal dinner which would be held in yet another town.

Steve's family was exhausted from driving all over the state in a 24-hour period, but they were good sports about it. They were lovely to my parents and seemed to genuinely enjoy meeting them. Nanny and my grandma got along very well. Steve's brother and uncle had already met Steve's other groomsmen on campus, so they felt more at ease.

The wedding day went without a hitch. Well, there was a bit of a panic when the ring bearer's suit didn't get picked up with the rest of the tuxes. The rental place was able to put the suit on a Greyhound bus at the last minute, and a driver was found to head to the nearest Greyhound stop to pick it up—again, a town 30 miles away.

My niece and nephew looked absolutely adorable in their outfits. He wore a tiny white tux with a sapphire cummerbund, and she wore a fluffy white satin dress overlaid with lace, trimmed with sapphire sash and ribbons. I wanted them to look like a tiny version of Steve and me and they nailed it. My sister-in-law did a beautiful job sewing my niece's dress.

Steve wore a white tux with a cutaway morning coat and cravat. He looked so handsome. When the wedding pictures came back, I could clearly see that he had indeed followed my instructions to wear white underwear and

It was a time of sweetness and discovery and a shiny new love that we thought would never break.

socks. Except the socks were white tube socks with red stripes. "Hey—they were the only white socks I had!" he protested. I was mad to begin with, but soon enough it turned into a funny story that we would retell and laugh about every time we looked at our wedding photos!

The music was beautiful. I walked down the aisle to Pachelbel's "Canon in D," played by euphonium, trumpet, and organ. Our friends sang. My brother and sister-in-law sang. Our friends broke into a spontaneous barber shop quartet during the reception and sang "Side By Side."

Due to threats of how they were going to decorate our car, we asked a man from the church to hide it for us. We'd had a hand in decorating other cars at other weddings, so we knew our friends had revenge plans for our car.

The nice man from church had a soft spot for me. As a teenager it was my job to clean the church every week. Whenever the vacuum acted up, and it did regularly, I called him, and he came to my rescue every time. He and his wife were kind to me. In fact, she attended my birth as one of my mom's nurses. He hid our car in his garage and even filled our gas tank that day. Whenever we went back to visit, we made sure to drop in and visit them, even when they didn't remember us very well anymore.

We drove off in our clean car with a full tank to begin our honeymoon. We spent a couple days in Minneapolis and then flew to Disney World.

I was amazed at everything I saw. Palm trees. The enormity of the theme park. Dinner in Cinderella's Castle. Finding a spot to ride out the thundershower every afternoon. Riding Space Mountain twice. Not having to look over my shoulder for someone reporting us for being without a chaperone.

It was a time of sweetness and discovery and a shiny new love that we thought would never break. Exactly as it should be in the early days of marriage.

19

Newlywed Bliss and Bats

OUR FIRST APARTMENT WAS A bit of a dump, but we could afford it and that's all that really mattered at the time. It was part of the second floor of an old character home not far from campus. It was furnished, which was very helpful to two college kids who didn't have much of anything to call our own. We had just enough money from wedding gifts to buy a bed and a TV.

We were working opposite hours. I worked days at the restaurant and Steve worked nights at the factory, while picking up shifts doing deliveries for a local furniture store.

I was still depressed, but I was managing it. It wasn't getting the best of me. I was able to go to work and socialize with friends, and enjoy being young and poor and in love with my husband. Things got complicated before too long, however.

Our town was in the middle of a migratory path for bats. As it was the middle of summer and we didn't have air conditioning, we put a box fan in the window of the bedroom for some relief from the heat. These two facts combined resulted in my spending the night in the middle of our bed under

Steve's golf umbrella, fighting off a bat with a flyswatter.

The next morning, Steve came home to a note on the door: "There's a bat!" He couldn't find it and we both hoped it had flown out the way it had flown in.

That day I prayed and "put out a fleece," like Gideon did in the Bible in Judges chapter 6. Instead of asking God to let the dew be only on the fleece and not on the ground, or let dew be only on the ground and not on the fleece, I told God if there were no bats the next night we would stay, but if there was another one, we would move. That night there were two bats.

I had not yet connected the dots that the fan was still in the window, providing more than enough room for a bat to get through. I also somewhat misunderstood the original purpose of putting out a fleece, but being the good Bible college girl I was, I interpreted this as a sign from God and started packing.

Our landlord, who lived downstairs, was upset that we were moving out. He liked us, and he liked that I vacuumed the main entrance and stairway. He was invested in trying to get us to stay.

When we told him there were two bats in the bedroom, he showed up drunk, in his not-quite-tied bathrobe, with a tennis racquet and a leather glove. He went into the bedroom, closed the door, and the banging and thumping began. He came out a few minutes later with a bat wing in his gloved hand. "I got one! The other one flew out the window."

He tried to convince us that bats were our friends. They ate the mosquitos that plagued our region every summer. He offered us a paper bag of freshly picked sweet corn. I was too busy packing to care, but I took the corn anyway. Hey—we were young and poor!

We moved that weekend into a new apartment building on the other side of town. Bye-bye bats, and bye-bye batty landlord.

Our old apartment had been furnished with old, moldering furniture, but it was a bonus since all we owned was a bed, a tv, a folding card table with four folding chairs, an old yellow swivel rocking chair from Steve's dorm room, and a two-shelf bookcase Steve paid a friend to make for me in college a couple years previously.

We got by. On the upside there was lots of room to invite friends over from campus for movie nights. They all brought pillows to make laying on the floor for a movie a little more comfortable.

I made the mistake of planning one of these parties on a Tuesday night without consulting my new husband. Not my smartest move. I had not yet caught on that Tuesday night was his only night to watch hockey on the limited channels we got. Steve came home to an apartment full of friends setting up a rented VCR. He got mad, went for a drive, and came back when he was feeling calmer. I learned two valuable lessons: I shouldn't invite people over without consulting my husband, and don't mess with Hockey Night.

On my days off work, I babysat for a neighbor across the hall looking after their cute little baby, Amanda. I enjoyed having her and initially didn't mind helping them out.

However, Amanda's dad got laid off, but didn't want to find another job unless it was a management position. He would drop the baby off to me in the morning so he could "job hunt." The baby would be dressed in yesterday's clothes, not bathed, and still wearing her night diaper. I was livid that this little girl wasn't being cared for properly at her home. I made it clear to him that I would not take her unless she had been bathed, fed, and changed into clean clothes.

Another day when I was watching Amanda, I heard her mother come home from work. The building wasn't very well insulated for sound—I heard the jangle of her keys, and their door opening and shutting. I waited over 30 minutes for her to come get the baby. I finally took Amanda across the hall and knocked on their door. The mother came to the door wondering why I was there. "I heard you come home over half an hour ago. I've been waiting for you to come pick her up."

"I'm not ready for her yet. I had a few things to do before I came to get her." Things like reading the mail, cleaning the tub, and who knows what else. Never mind I had done all those things at my place while looking after her baby.

That was the end of babysitting for them. I felt terrible for the baby, but I had to draw the line. I learned that although I thought I was being a good neighbor by not charging for childcare, they did not appreciate the value I added to their life. I think that may have been my first lesson about boundaries.

Our first Christmas together was also a time of establishing boundaries. It was important to me to create our own Christmas traditions. Of course, we would go to the farm for Christmas day and visit with family. But I wanted us to have our own Christmas Eve tradition, starting with our first Christmas as a married couple.

We were too poor to have a Christmas tree, but we did have a hand-me-down three tier wooden plant stand, so we decorated that. We bought a few cheap ornaments to start an ornament collection that was only ours. I am still very fond of those little shepherds and angels!

I made a special meal. I roasted Cornish hens, along with potatoes and carrots and the crescent rolls you pop out of a can. Cornish hens remain our Christmas Eve dinner of choice, and while I prefer a better-quality dinner roll, it's tradition now to bake the canned ones. After dinner Steve and I opened our few gifts and watched a Christmas movie.

We joined my family the next day. My mom was a bit put out that we hadn't come for Christmas Eve and stayed overnight. When I explained my desire to create our own traditions from the beginning, she said, "I guess that makes sense. You always had to be different than your brothers and sisters." Her tone sounded like she meant it as a criticism, but I took it as a compliment.

As the new year began, I was back at college to complete my last semester required to graduate. I went to the new Dean of Students and asked, "What do I need to do to get out of here with a degree?" An English minor was added to my music minor and Bible major, and I looked forward to my graduation in May 1988.

20

Remembering

BEING A MARRIED STUDENT WAS very different from living on campus. I was free of dorm drama. I could come and go without signed permission passes. Our apartment was a popular off-campus destination for our friends.

I had to scale back on work hours during the school year, so we struggled to meet rent and bills. At one point I called an uncle and he very kindly gave us enough money to meet rent that month.

And the memories came crashing in like a tsunami.

Another Sunday after church, I opened the cupboard to see what I could make for lunch. We had one can of soup, a few stale crackers, and a bit of rice. With a week until the next payday, I didn't know how we were going to eat, but I prayed God would provide.

A moment later there was a knock on the door. Steve's old roommate and best friend was there with his arms full of a bucket of fried chicken and all the sides. "Lunch on campus is gross today. Can I eat with you guys?" He left all the leftovers and we made them last until payday on Friday. We also received an anonymous check in the mail which came at the perfect time and for which we were extremely grateful.

My depression hadn't been an issue for quite awhile. I was busy with school, busy with work, in love with my husband, and hosting movie/popcorn nights for friends. I was feeling good about life and our future together, until my world imploded one afternoon.

I was making Kraft Dinner with hotdogs for supper. I was expecting Steve home from work soon. The TV was on, airing the Oprah Winfrey show in the other room. I listened in as I cooked.

Oprah was interviewing a guest and talking about child sexual abuse, how it was underreported and misunderstood. The damage, they said, could last a lifetime if not treated.

I turned off the stove. I walked zombie-like into the living room. And the memories came crashing in like a tsunami.

Him tweaking my cheek.

Begging to go home with him for the afternoon.

Holding his hand as we walked to his home.

Sitting on his lap with the guitar.

Running away, leaving my shoes behind.

Standing scared in Grandma's kitchen.

Walking back in only my socks.

Hiding under the weeping willow tree.

It didn't happen it didn't happen it didn't happen.

Yelled at and spanked for my ruined socks.

When Steve got home, he found me curled up in the corner, in a fetal position, chanting, "It didn't happen it didn't happen it didn't happen."

I told him everything.

He was horrified and scared for me. He wanted to help, but didn't know how.

The nightmares started again. Never about the molestation, always about siblings seeing me hurt or scared or needing rescue, laughing at me. These nightmares occurred almost every night, often ending only when I woke up screaming.

I couldn't sleep. I couldn't focus on studying. Somehow, I managed to graduate, but I have no idea how, stuck in a haze of unreality and recurring trauma responses.

21

Confronting My Parents

STEVE ENCOURAGED ME TO GO home and confront my parents. I was devastated by the memory of my initial disclosure that had resulted in my mother telling me she didn't "have time for this" and walking away to do the laundry. I fully believed this memory to be true, as it made sense in light of what I knew of my mother and how she reacted to me.

My mother walking away from me completely confirmed what I already knew to be true—I was never wanted. I garnered approval if and when I behaved within expectations. They were thrilled to finally have me out of the house and enjoyed their empty nest. Even now, she was annoyed when I called home and wanted to talk longer than five minutes. These were the perceptions that were my reality. I was getting very tired of trying to win her love.

We picked a weekend and went home to the farm. During the previous few years, my parents had been going through the incredibly difficult process of bankruptcy resulting in the loss of our second-generation family farm. They were still living on the farm property, but now it was owned by someone else and they were paying rent to live in the home they had previously owned and where they had raised their family for nearly 40 years. This arrangement lasted until they chose to move into town.

That Saturday I sat at the table with my mom. "I have something I need to talk to you about, that happened to me when I was little."

Her eyes teared up. "I know exactly what you are about to say. It's about ____, isn't it?"

I was shocked. "You remember??"

"I never forgot. It made me sick to have to take communion from him every month. It still does."

"I don't understand. When I told you, you said you were busy doing laundry. Nothing was ever done about it."

Her eyes flew open wide. "That's not what happened at all! You told me in the car on the way home from town that he touched you. When we got home, I brought you outside to weed the flower bed because that's the only place I knew the other kids wouldn't bother us. You told me everything. You cried and clung to me and begged me, saying, "Mommy, please don't make me talk about it again. I just want to forget."

"I told your father, and he thought it was best to let you do just that," she continued. "After all, children who said these kinds of things weren't believed in those days. And if it got out to the community, it would destroy the reputation of the church, not to mention the family. He is a deacon after all."

I was speechless. I didn't remember any of that. I did, however, have a faint memory of talking about it in the car, which didn't jive with my memory of telling her in the kitchen. I decided she must be telling the truth.

So many conflicting thoughts collided in my mind.

Dad is a man of faith, and he prays about important decisions. He must have prayed about it and truly believed it was in my best interests to stay silent.

They may not have charged my molester, but once they knew what he did to me they must have been keeping a close eye on him over the years to make sure he didn't hurt anyone else.

But he was an elementary school janitor—for so many years. And there was that one girl from the community who accused him. The church defended him; my parents included. This was after they knew what he did to me. Was he innocent that time? Or did they cover up for him just to preserve the church's reputation in the community, like Mom said?

When that girl came forward, why wasn't he charged? Why wasn't she protected and defended by a body of believers who claim to worship God? Why wasn't he charged when I came forward? Even if I wasn't believed in court, I would have felt believed and supported by my family.

I talked to Dad about it later that day. He was confused. He didn't remember ever knowing about it.

This was the worst thought of all. My molestation was so insignificant to him that he didn't even remember it. He showed little concern. When I asked Mom about this, she said, "You know your father. He forgets things. Out of sight out of mind."

I felt diminished. I felt disposable. And now on top of my complete lack of self esteem and depression, I was dealing with PTSD. I didn't know it at the time—it remained undiagnosed until 1996, but that's what it was. Every time I was triggered the brokenness was driven further into my brain.

Now, in the present day, after talking it through with a trusted niece, I think that Mom didn't actually tell him. My niece remembers a grandpa who loved her completely, just as he loved all his grandkids. He was also a man of deep integrity. There was no way her grandpa would learn about what happened to me and not go scorched earth on the guy who molested his daughter.

This rang true. I remembered the man begging me not to tell my dad or my grandpa. He was literally on his knees, pleading with me, practically in tears. He was terrified of what they would do to him if they knew.

I believe she's right—Dad never knew. Mom kept it to herself, operating from a place of fear and shame. That explains her comments about the reputation of the church and the family. She lied to me.

I still struggle with that. I choose to forgive her, but the damage remains. She believed that I was an acceptable sacrifice on the altar of religious reputation. Letting that man go free to continue to molest other little girls was better than risking the church's standing in the community, especially since the church had defended him against similar accusations. Message received.

I asked for a meeting with the pastor that same afternoon that I talked

---

I know for certain I'm not the only one who was molested in that church.

with my parents. I told him the story of what happened to me and named the pedophile who still attended the church. I made him promise to watch that perpetrator and not let him near any of the children.

"He's very old, and can barely walk, even with the help of a cane. He has terminal cancer. I don't think he's much of a threat," said the pastor.

"He has always portrayed himself as feeble," I answered. "That's how pedophiles get away with their crimes for so long. They are very good at presenting themselves as completely harmless, so people lower their guard around them. I don't buy it for a minute," I insisted. "As long as he is breathing, he is a threat and you need to take this warning seriously."

The pastor promised me he would keep an eye on him and keep him away from the children in his congregation, I think just to get me out of his office.

I really don't know if he took me seriously. But I did what I could do and had to leave the rest in God's hands.

To this day, I don't know if my molester victimized any of the other girls in the church. I do know, from talking to my childhood friends, that he was warned by a couple of my friends' fathers about "inappropriate behavior" toward their daughters. He was spoken to severely enough that he stayed away from those girls from then on.

I also now know that he wasn't the only pedophile in the church. There was another man, a boys' Sunday School teacher, which worked out nicely for him, since he preferred little boys, while my molester preferred little girls. They stayed out of each other's way, and had an agreement of sorts that amounted to mutually assured destruction if either of them told on the other.

I know for certain I'm not the only one who was molested in that church. All I can do is pray that the other victims find healing and peace, and offer my support if they need it.

22

Moving to New Ulm

I WENT BACK TO MY life. I went to work and did all my normal activities. Steve was working out of town and only home on the weekends. I missed him. The loneliness exacerbated my depression. The nightmares continued. I was falling apart but didn't know how to ask for help. I didn't know I could ask for help beyond talking to yet another pastor.

Only crazy people went to a therapist, and that stigma kept me from seeking help, even if we could have afforded it, which we couldn't. We were barely making rent and paying for groceries. I thought about suicide a lot. But now I was married, and I didn't want to put Steve through that. He was freaked out by the nightmares, there's no way I could put him through my suicide. He was the only one I could talk to and he couldn't fix it, which frustrated us both. So, I did what I always did—sucked it up and pretended to be ok.

I flushed my birth control pills on our first anniversary. I thought everything would be okay, and I would finally be happy, if only I could get pregnant. That would fix me. I would be a wonderful mother. I would tell my baby every day how much I loved them. My baby would love me back. Everything would be fine. I could still get my fairy-tale happy ending.

I was an idiot.

Steve got hired by UPS as a delivery driver for the 1987 Christmas rush. His performance got him a permanent full-time position. However, they needed him in New Ulm, Minnesota, about an hour away from where we were living. I was finishing my last semester at college. My parents knew a pastor in New Ulm. I reached out, and they agreed to let Steve stay with them during the week, and he came home on weekends. With only one car to share, there was a lot of driving back and forth on Fridays and Sundays.

We finally moved to New Ulm after my graduation in 1988. We found a mostly furnished second-floor apartment in an old square three-story brick building. Our landlady had the first floor. We had half of the second floor, and a young mom lived on the third floor. I tried making friends with her, but she had no interest.

I found work as a nanny for a single dad in the church. Three kids, aged 13 and younger. Sweet kids. They were obviously lacking a mother figure, as their mom lived on the other side of the country.

I played games with them. Took them to the neighborhood pool. Cooked meals. Cleaned the house. We baked together. I once asked them if they wanted to lick the beater when we were making a cake.

"What's a beater?"

"You've never licked a beater before?"

Two little heads shook no. My heart broke a little.

I tried tutoring the youngest. She was nearing school age and her dad wanted me to teach her to read. That didn't go well. She spent most of her time chewing on her hair. I couldn't keep her attention because I didn't know what I was doing and I had no business trying to be a teacher.

Apparently, their mom was making moves to challenge custody. The dad panicked. He wanted to run with the kids and asked me to go with him so I could continue caring for them and tutoring them.

I got a creepy vibe off this guy. My concern for the kids was the only thing keeping me there. But when he asked me to run away with him with his kids?? That was a hard no and a huge red flag. I told Steve, we told the pastor, and I quit.

The oldest boy was old enough to make up his own mind where he wanted to live. His dad was trying to bribe him with a new stereo he had been asking for. He was also worried about leaving his little brother and sister behind. He and I had a long talk. I told him to go live with his mom. His dad was verbally abusive toward him—it was only a matter of time before it got physical.

"You need to save yourself," I told him. "Once you are at your mom's you can tell your lawyer to tell the judge what's going on. Then they can get your brother and sister out of there."

I felt I should call child services. The pastor counseled me against it. "The government doesn't know what is best for these children. They could end up in a non-Christian foster home. We will pray for them that God will keep them safe."

One of my biggest regrets is that I didn't follow my gut and make the call. I fell for the "circle the holy wagons" strategy. Over the years I have learned this is a favorite solution among fundamentalists. The us-against-them mentality is very prevalent. And it puts the most vulnerable at risk. It put those kids at risk. Being in a "non-Christian" foster home might have meant they didn't go to church three times a week, but it also might have meant they were safe.

I still remember their names. I still pray for them. And I beg forgiveness for not standing in the gap for them when they needed someone to step up.

We were in New Ulm for a few months when Steve's file ended up on the right desk at just the right time. UPS discovered Steve was a Canadian with leadership experience from his student government involvement in college. UPS had expanded into Canada and they wanted to train Canadians for executive positions so their expansion teams could return to the US. They asked him if he had ever considered Human Resources as a career path and offered him training.

I yelled WAHOO! and started packing. Winnipeg, here we come!

23

Moving to Winnipeg

WE MOVED TO WINNIPEG IN October 1988, after Steve completed his HR training in Toronto. The day we got possession of our rented townhome Steve got sent to Thunder Bay on a business trip.

So I, the unaccompanied illegal alien just beginning the process of becoming a landed immigrant, was left sitting at the customs office, unable to access our moving van filled with all our possessions, including our car, waiting for my Canadian husband to sign for it so the lock on the back of the van could be removed by Customs and Immigration officials. Except that my Canadian husband was already on a plane to Ontario. They had no idea what to do with me, and it was becoming increasingly awkward for them to have me sitting in their waiting room all day and to have my moving van clogging up their parking lot. They finally allowed me to sign for our goods after many phone calls to UPS, phone calls to superior customs officials, and warnings to me about not misrepresenting myself and my purpose for seeking landed immigrant status.

I learned a valuable lesson that day. No need to argue and fight for what I need. Just sit patiently until everyone feels awkward and they finally give in.

This has proven to be an effective strategy in many situations.

The moving guys were extremely helpful and kind enough to be sure the bed was put together for me. I gave them Subway sandwiches and fell into bed, sleeping through an eight inch snow dump overnight.

My first morning in my new home, in a new city, in a new country, where I knew no one except my husband, who wasn't there. I felt overwhelmed with loneliness.

The cable hadn't been hooked up so there was no TV to keep me company. I dug through the unpacked boxes until I found my clock radio. I plugged it in, set the local time, and started scanning radio stations. It took a minute to find one that wasn't French speaking. I started unpacking boxes and settling into my new home.

Necessity is the mother of invention.

I was soon feeling appropriately sorry for myself and picked up the phone to call my mom before I remembered our phone hadn't been hooked up yet. Now I was truly annoyed—I couldn't even complain to my mom about all the injustices of my new life in Canada. At least I had my car now and could go for a drive.

Nope. Eight inches of snow. No snow shovel. Not even a pet to keep me company!!! One of my dad's favorite sayings came to me in that moment: Necessity is the mother of invention.

That car was going to get dug out one way or another. I scanned my belongings for anything I could use to move snow. One cookie sheet and 20 minutes later, I was wheels on the road. Two of my new neighbors were startled by my cookie sheet shovel and gave me a wide berth. A third applauded my ingenuity and offered me the use of his shovel, but I was finished by then.

Job one, fill the gas tank.

Job two, buy a snow shovel.

Job three, start learning my way around my new city.

I decided the best way to learn my way around was to get lost and find my way home again. I did have a map but used it as little as possible. I wanted to explore. I discovered my local grocery store. I found McDonald's. Note to self: be sure to tell my mom to tell my nephews about McDonald's, as they were genuinely concerned there may be no Happy Meals in Canada.

Fun fact about grocery shopping in Canada: because there are two official languages, French and English, all labels are printed with both. It took a couple grocery adventures before I figured out all I had to do was turn the box or can around on the shelf to read the English label. I was a little slow on the uptake sometimes. In fact, I got so frustrated by not being able to read product labels that I got a headache every time I went shopping, which led me to the pharmacy aisle where I learned they didn't sell Advil over the counter in Canada. These were my first world immigrant problems.

I was still struggling with my mental health and still having nightmares with the repeating theme of me needing rescue and my siblings laughing at me. I called back home, and sometimes called a sibling or two, to try to stay in touch. I often wished when the phone rang it would be one of them calling me for a change. I tired of being the only one to reach out and I stopped trying after a while. The message was clear. The Canadian border created a relational boundary. This was not an assumption. I was told more than once, "Well, you are the one who moved to Canada." Apparently, that disconnect applied to letters as well, not just long-distance international phone calls.

I also struggled a lot with PMS. It was getting steadily worse month by month. I suspect now that I had endometriosis. I didn't know anything about it at the time and no doctor suggested diagnostics to find out. Endometriosis explains the severe pain, bloating, and dramatic mood swings. That, combined with depression, resulted in my being a mess more days than not.

We were also trying to conceive. It wasn't going well. Steve was traveling for work nearly three weeks out of every month. We were emotionally disconnected. I was feeling sick or depressed most of the time. I expected Steve to love me enough to make it all better. I created an impossible set of expectations, and then resented him for not meeting them.

The feelings of loneliness and worthlessness and abandonment grew deeper. My family only connected with me if I made the effort. My husband only connected with me between work trips and TV sports. I didn't know how to cope so I spent hours at a time playing video games to numb out. Thanks, Nintendo, for *Legend of Zelda*.

I was also deeply upset that I couldn't get pregnant. Everywhere I looked I saw pregnant women. There were baby showers at church that I was expected to attend, and it was becoming increasingly difficult to fake my smile through those celebrations. One night on the news there was a report of a baby being found in a dumpster behind a low rent apartment building. That broke me. It was time to tell God exactly what I thought.

Really God? Every child is a gift from You, right? That person deserved the gift of a child and I don't? Seriously though! That person literally threw their baby in the trash, and you decided they get to get pregnant and I don't? I would have loved that baby. I would have taken good care of that baby. I would have given ANYTHING to be able to raise that baby. But no. You let it get thrown in the dumpster to die in the middle of winter. And I'm supposed to love you and trust your will for my life???

And while we are on the topic, GOD, it's time to hash out a few things.

You gave me to a family that didn't want me, and still doesn't.

Your Bible tells me you will give me the desires of my heart. All I ever wanted was to be a mommy—YOU put that desire in my heart from the time I was a toddler. And you continue to deny me, giving babies to people who throw them away. That's clearly a better option than letting me be a mother, in your opinion.

You let me get molested at 6 years old and let the deacon who did it get away with it, along with countless other sexual predator crimes.

I did everything you ever wanted. I was a good little Christian girl who went to church, carried her Bible to school, and graduated not only from Christian high school but also Christian college. I married a Bible college guy and I was still a virgin. Well, except for my molester, so maybe I wasn't, but that wasn't my choice. I sing at church and teach Sunday school. I kept my side of the bargain. It's time you do the same.

But you are God. You have all the power. I have none. Message received. When you said you love the whole world you forgot about me. Now you are stuck with me. You have to love me, but you don't have to like me. You are just like everyone else. I'm just not good enough.

Sometimes the despair was so deep I couldn't see daylight anymore. Just darkness. With no hope in sight. My thought life was regularly invaded by suicide ideation.

24

My Parents' Origin Stories

WE HAD BEEN LIVING IN Winnipeg for about a year, but I wasn't working yet because I was waiting for my landed immigrant status. Dad called me on the phone.

That NEVER happened. It scared me a little, to be honest.

Dad had been hired as foreman of a construction crew that was building a new church, but it was a couple hours away from home. He had reached the point where he was so concerned about Mom's state of mind that he emptied the medicine cabinet into a bag, along with every kitchen knife, every time he left the house, even for only a half hour.

He explained how losing the farm had triggered her about losing their home when she was very young. He told me the story. So many things clicked into place for me. Why she would get mad when she caught me looking through the Sears Christmas Wish Book. How she would drag me by the arm away from shop windows because we couldn't afford what I saw, so there was no point in even looking. Her mounting anxiety over the years about children to feed and clothe, and her crippling fear over losing the farm. It all made sense for the very first time.

"Why did she never tell me about this?"

"She was ashamed," Dad answered.

Tears flooded my eyes as my heart broke for that sweet little girl who was so terribly wounded, never fully healed, and still living in shame over things that were, then and now, utterly out of her control.

Dad now needed to be on the building site for days at a time. And he desperately needed this job. "I need you to come home and look after Mom for me."

I was aware of the events of the previous years that resulted in bankruptcy and loss of the family farm. The 1980's was a bad time for family farms, dairy farmers in particular, and things hadn't improved much over time for my parents.

It all became too much for Mom to deal with and she broke down. She tried Prozac after fighting with the doctor over it. She had a bad reaction, flushed them, and refused any further treatment. Knowing what I know now about Prozac and my mom, I heartily agree with her choice to not take it. Further psychological treatment was inaccessible in their small community, and she flatly refused to engage in any kind of counseling beyond their pastor. She leaned on Dad, the church, and her closest friends.

But she was struggling hard and Dad had to work, this time away from home. So when he called for help, of course I went. I stayed with Mom on the farm for a few weeks until Dad finished his foreman job.

I had learned a lot about Mom over the years, and the time spent alone with her on the farm during her breakdown brought all the stories into sharp focus.

Mom grew up the third child of four in a tumultuous home. Her father was British in every sense of the word. His word was law and no one dared challenge it. He served every dish at dinner from his place at the head of the table. He was often unkind and frequently abusive. Mom overheard many arguments and saw worse.

When Mom was about 5 years old, her father lost his job but didn't tell the family. He got up every morning, dressed in his suit, put on his hat, grabbed his briefcase, and went out the door to "work" as a premium collector for an insurance company. A few months went by until one day the sheriff came to the door. He nailed an eviction notice to the front door and gave my grandmother a limited number of hours to save from her belongings whatever personal items she wanted to keep. The rest belonged to the bank. The hours went by far too quickly. My mom sat on cartons of their essentials that they piled at the curb, watching as the pile of boxes and suitcases grew around her, supervised by police officers.

When time was up, the door was locked, and the family was literally on the street, with no explanation as to why the bank repossessed their home. Eventually Grandpa came home, finding them there.

I don't know what happened after that. Obviously, they found some kind of shelter, and eventually a different place to live, albeit in a much poorer neighborhood.

Mom once told me how they would escape the house and go the "the main drag" in their neighborhood. They would go to the big window at the diner, pressed their saddest and hungriest looking faces up against the window, and then scamper away once they were shooed off by the owner. Sometimes, a tender-hearted patron would buy them a little something and send it out to them. But that only happened at the beginning, until they began to be recognized. She laughed and her face shone with girlish delight and mischief as she recalled that story.

Mom once told me she felt embarrassed every time she became pregnant.

119

She felt people were judging her. I didn't understand then, but now it's not hard to figure it out.

Mom was pregnant when they got married. I never saw her through a lens of shame because of that, but she saw herself that way. To be honest, given her upbringing and lack of education about her body, an unplanned pregnancy was not an unexpected outcome.

When she got her first period, she was terrified and thought she was dying. Her brother explained what was happening and bought the necessary hygiene products she needed. She should have learned about it from her mother, but those things were considered shameful and weren't talked about.

But that was where her education stopped. She wasn't taught about sex, or conception, or birth control. Those things were shrouded in shame and secrecy. When I think about how vulnerable she was, because of a code of silence around "things that just weren't talked about," I feel angry. That code of silence trapped her in a cycle of shame that continued throughout her life, and it didn't need to be that way.

Mom's sister went to college where she met the man she would marry, who coincidentally was my dad's brother. When Dad came out to Detroit to serve as best man for his brother, he met and fell in love with my mom, who was maid of honor for her sister. They were deeply and truly in love. Dad moved from the farm to Detroit over the winter and worked in a factory. During that time they dated and he lived with my mom's family. Eventually the abuses Mom was suffering came to light and Dad wanted to rescue her, but she was only 17 and needed to finish high school.

Summer came again and Dad headed back to the family farm in Minnesota to help with planting and tending the crops. When the school year ended Mom went west to visit her newly married sister, who lived near Dad's family farm. Summertime on the prairies fosters all kinds of growth, including my parents' love for each other. Mom went back to Detroit, Dad followed after the harvest season, going back to work in the factory for the winter.

Dad asked for permission to marry Mom, but was denied by her father. Mom was in her senior year of high school. The clock was ticking down until she was 18 and could marry him without her parents' permission, but they wanted to ensure her parents' cooperation. A pregnancy was a reasonable exit strategy. She got pregnant in the winter, graduated, and married in May of 1950.

She wore a lovely off-white organza knee-length dress. She told me her family couldn't afford a wedding gown, which is why she wore that dress instead. I knew the real reason was the pregnancy, because when I asked why they could afford a wedding gown for her sister but not her, she refused to talk about it any further.

I think she should have been allowed to wear a blindingly white, full length wedding gown with a cathedral length train. She deserved to experience that magical bride feeling as she stepped into an exquisite satin gown made just for her, gliding down the aisle as she peered demurely through the veil, basking in the glow of her love's adoration.

Instead, along with a bouquet, she carried fear and shame and anxiety down the aisle, worried that she might already be showing and people would know she was pregnant. I think she also carried hope. Hope that her life could be different now. She could leave the home where she had witnessed and suffered abuse. She could live in another state with the man she loved, learn to be a good farm wife, and leave the pain and shame behind. This is all speculation, of course, because I have only my own imaginings for reference. But my heart wants her to be happy and hopeful on her wedding day.

My parents honeymooned at Niagara Falls, and then started their life at a small farm in southern Minnesota, not far from Dad's father's farm. Dad worked with his father running the dairy operation. Mom learned to keep house, cook, and sew from her mother-in-law.

My parents were the subject of a lot of gossip because of the pregnancy. In fact, they were outright shunned in the community. Mom suffered the brunt of it, because she was the woman, carrying the evidence of their shame right out front for all to see.

It never made sense to me that she carried such deep shame over the community's disapproval of her. I mean, in the beginning, sure. It would have been difficult to be the city girl moving to the farm, literally as a teenage bride. No electricity, no plumbing, baby on the way, scraping a living from the ground. Add a baby born on the "wrong side of the blanket" and trying to fit in to the legalistic fundamentalist Baptist church? That kind of pressure is crippling to a young wife.

There was an interdenominational community choir when my parents were first married—a gathering of all the church choirs in town. Since both my parents were good singers, they decided to join the choir and showed up for rehearsal. One of the women spoke out publicly against my mom that night, stating, "If she is allowed to sing, I'm leaving." A few other women agreed, and my parents decided to leave rather than cause a scene.

The older people in the church never let my parents forget their "sin." This kind of shaming was not unusual. The fact that she was pregnant before they were married was a stain on their reputation that Mom was never able to be rid of. Dad was not allowed to be a deacon in that church for almost 40 years. That's how long it took for the old guard to die off. For some reason, my dad was able to let the judgement and disapproval roll off him, but Mom was unable to do that. That's pretty hard to do when you get pregnant every year and, instead of congratulations, you get "You're pregnant AGAIN??" The memory of her shame was resurrected year after year with each new pregnancy.

Years later, as a teenager, when I finally did the math and realized that my oldest sibling was the same age as the years they had been married, Mom was amused that it took me that long to figure it out. But her laughter soon turned to tears that afternoon as she felt the weight of shame all over again. I didn't care that she was pregnant before she was married. I cared deeply, however, that she still carried the stigma of being ostracized by the community.

It didn't bother my dad that the old cronies were still condemning them. In fact, he was inordinately proud of the fact that they had produced nine kids. He loved quoting a verse from Psalms—something about a man being happy with a full quiver. He said having a full quiver meant having six arrows, and he had nine, so he had a quiver and a half!

My experience with Mom in those few weeks at the farm changed my life.

Mom just rolled her eyes at him—it was easy for him to boast about having nine kids when he hadn't been pregnant for a total of 81 months, given birth nine times, and been the primary caregiver to raise them all.

I like to imagine that every time there was another baby on the way, Dad saw it as a passive-aggressive way to stick it to the critics. The harder they judged, the prouder he got. I don't know that to be exactly true, but it's not hard to imagine Dad feeling that way, reading between the lines.

I do wish Mom had had autonomy over her reproductive health during those years. She told me she wouldn't go on the pill before I was born, because Dad didn't want her to, and a good Christian wife obeys her husband no matter what.

My experience with Mom in those few weeks at the farm changed my life.

I knew her in a way that she had never revealed to me before. She struggled for hours just to get out of bed. She would go into the kitchen to make coffee, but could not remember how. She was afraid of getting the mail. I made the coffee. I made the meals, although it was a fight to get her to eat anything. I got the mail. I sat with her on her bed in the morning for as long as it took for her to be able to get up. I listened. I loved on her as much as I possibly could.

I rebuked her every time she apologized to me for being in that condition. "Mom, please don't apologize. I get it. I really and truly understand."

"I know you do. I remember how hard it was for you during high school. I'm glad you're here."

She felt humiliated about being seen in her condition and we never talked about it again. It was one more thing she felt shame about.

I could relate. I was feeling shame too. Despite a deep desire to be a mommy, I couldn't conceive.

25

Infertility

PREGNANCY JUST WASN'T HAPPENING FOR us, so we looked into adoption. We contacted Child & Family Services (CFS) and made an appointment with an adoption worker. We were told it would be up to seven years if we wanted an infant. We could have a child almost immediately if we were able to take an older special needs child.

My heart was torn.

I wanted to take every child that needed a home. But of course that wasn't

---

I yelled at God a lot those days.

reasonable or practical. I had no experience or training with special needs. We felt it would be unfair to a child to be placed with parents that didn't have the experience, ability, or financial resources to care properly for ongoing specialized care.

And, I'll be honest—I desperately wanted the newborn experience. I couldn't let that go. I was already missing out on the pregnancy experience. I hoped God didn't hold it against me and that all the children already waiting would find loving homes.

We completed the filing requirements and began our wait.

Another period.

Another heartbreak.

Another round of yelling at God. I yelled at God a lot those days.

And suddenly, a question occurred to me. If I was unhappy with a seven-year wait, and never knowing anything about the birthparents, were there birth moms who were equally unhappy with this system? What did they do? Where did they go? Were there other resources for them?

This was pre-Google, so all I had to work with were the white pages and the yellow pages. I looked up every key word I could think of. There was nothing under adoption except CFS. However, when I looked up pregnancy, I found an agency called Crisis Pregnancy Centre. I called them and explained my situation. "Are there any resources available to pregnant girls other than CFS?"

"Funny you should ask. Just a few months ago a new adoption facilitation service, Adoption Options, moved in on the floor below us."

"I looked up adoption in the phone book but didn't find them," I replied.

"They are so new they aren't in the phone book yet. Would you like their number?"

"Yes, please!"

And so began a new journey of renewed hope.

Steve and I talked about next steps. I was ready to roll—he was apprehensive. In our relationship, I am always the one ready to jump in the deep end and worry about the water wings later. Steve has always been the one to ask the important questions first.

I didn't want to ask the questions because I didn't want to discover I didn't like the answers. I just wanted to be happy and thought having a baby would fix me, and this felt like a good solution. But I knew if I pushed too hard, he would come to a full stop on the issue. I had to be patient and give him space to make up his own mind without feeling pressured.

I didn't do that very well. I can be patient, but only sometimes and in very specific situations. This wasn't one of those situations.

After a couple weeks, Steve decided he was ready to take the next step—calling for more information. They mailed out an information packet, explaining how private adoption worked in Manitoba. If we wanted to pursue private adoption through Adoption Options, we had to register for a $650 weekend seminar. The next one was in October, a few months away.

Well, that put a damper on my enthusiasm. I had no idea how we were going to come up with that kind of money. In 1990, that was nearly a month's rent. Steve said, "Let's not give up yet. Let's pray about it and see what happens."

I had been praying about lots of things, and by praying, I mean I spent a lot of time yelling at God. I was not convinced He was in a charitable mood, at least not toward me.

Steve had been promoted at UPS and was working as an HR supervisor. He was still traveling frequently and had an expense account. Shortly after our prayer for money, he went to the office and there on his desk was an overdue expense reimbursement for $650—the exact amount we needed.

We knew for sure it was God. I mean, c'mon—what expense reimbursement check had ever been for an exact dollar amount? Usually it's a random amount, like $432.79, or something like that. Nope—this one was $650 even. The exact amount we needed at the exact time we needed it. The deadline to register for the next weekend seminar was almost up. Steve took the check to the bank, I cried, he laughed, and we mailed in our registration.

This was October 1990. I had finally gotten my landed immigrant status and was working as a manager at a women's gym. I had to miss work the Saturday of the adoption orientation weekend. My boss wasn't impressed, because she had to cover for me, but I didn't care. Let them fire me. It was worth it; I could get another job. And once we ended up with a baby, I was going to be a stay-at-home mom anyway.

The Friday night session involved a get-to-know-you time, as well as a discussion about how open adoption worked. The two facilitators introduced themselves and told their adoption stories, explaining how they came to open Adoption Options in Winnipeg, an expansion of the first office in Calgary, Alberta.

They explained how the weekend would unfold. Saturday was a long day with a lot of content to digest. They brought in an adoption attorney to teach us about the legal process and to answer any questions. I was relieved to learn that the fact I was still an American wouldn't be an issue.

There was a presentation by an adoptive couple and their baby, along with their birth mom, who had previously gone through Adoption Options. This session had the most impact on me.

I was amazed at how easily the baby was passed from mom to dad to birth mom and back again. They were just normal people, treating one another with obvious affection and respect, all with the same goal of providing love and security and family for this little girl.

We learned that the relationship had started slowly, but progressed to a more open and comfortable friendship, which turned into their "chosen family." They met regularly for dinner, the birth mom occasionally baby-sat and was included in all her birth daughter's special moments, like birthdays and holiday events.

This was even more than I could have ever dreamed! I could have a chosen family where I felt appreciated and respected by a birth mom who might come to like me? My heart raced at the potential opportunity to build a family of our own that included a birth mom who actively participated in our child's life.

We still had some fears to face. Not every match followed through to a successful adoption. There was a window of time where the birth mom could change her mind and take the baby back. As difficult as that scenario was to contemplate, it's only fair. A woman deserves the time she needs to be sure of her decision.

We understood the risks, but we were convinced this was the path God had given us. We would build our family through adoption.

There were no further fees going forward. We completed our file, including pictures, our bios, and a Dear Birthmother letter, introducing ourselves and describing our life and what we could offer a child.

That was a hard letter to write. How do you say, "Dear Birthmother, we are infertile and we want your baby?" What are the right things to include about us and our life? We planned to raise our child in the Christian faith. What if someone looking for a home for her baby got freaked out by how often we went to church? (To be honest, it kinda freaked me out sometimes, how high the expectations for attendance and serving were in our fundamentalist Baptist church.)

What if she wanted someone who owned a home—we were still renting. What if we didn't make enough money? All the what-ifs kept circling our brains. All we could do was tell the truth and let God take care of the rest. We finished our file by the end of the month, it was officially activated, and we began the wait.

There are many key differences between closed government adoption and open private adoption.

Government adoption is a first-come, first-served system. They do all the background checks and home studies while you wait your turn in a very long line.

Identities are removed from all communication. The birth mother has no idea or control over where her baby will be placed. She must accept a life of never knowing where her child is, if the child is okay, or even if the child is still alive. The records remain closed.

Private open adoption is very different. The birth mother has all the control. She decides what kind of parents she wants her baby to have and has access to all the active files. It is a long, arduous process, including multiple visits to the Adoption Options office and Crisis Pregnancy Centre. She undergoes counseling to be sure she is making her decision of her own free will. She learns all about the legal process, so she knows her rights and the rights of the adoptive parents. She is given a facilitator who offers support and guidance throughout the entire process.

We felt much more comfortable with open adoption because of all the care and support given to the birth mom. We hoped we would eventually develop a loving relationship with her. We didn't know if or how that would happen. We were taking a big leap of faith, hoping for the best.

26

Adoption Options

WHILE WE WAITED, I VOLUNTEERED at Adoption Options on my days off work from the gym. I did basic admin stuff—dealt with the mail, kept the database up to date, and answered the phone.

One of my main tasks was to field requests for information from potential birth mothers and people wanting to adopt. I would talk to the person seeking more information and then compile an information package for them. I usually mailed them out on my way home at the end of the day.

There were very strict rules about volunteering at AO. They couldn't be perceived to be favoring the volunteers who were actively waiting over the waiting couples who didn't volunteer.

Whenever a potential birth mom was scheduled to come in, they gave me enough notice so I could use the bathroom, because once the potential birth mom arrived, I was stuck in the back office. I was not to be seen or heard in case it would look like I was getting preferential treatment.

One of the facilitators had recently adopted a baby girl, and sometimes she brought her baby to the office. Those were my favorite days because I got to look after her. Having a baby in the office was usually a delightful thing, until the day it was a very sad thing.

I was there the day an adoptive couple and their young son came in with their baby, who had been placed with them several months previously. The birth mother had revoked her consent to adopt, so they had to relinquish the baby back to the birth mom. The exchange was happening that day in our office.

The little family brought in boxes and bags of things that belonged to the baby—everything from the car seat and stroller to clothes and toys. It was unbelievably heart-breaking to watch them say goodbye to their baby, hand him over, and leave with empty arms and broken hearts, tears streaming down

We couldn't shake the feeling that God was in control, and it was going to be okay.

their faces as they tried to explain to their son why his brother wasn't going home with them.

I helped look after the baby until the birth mom arrived. She didn't even look at the baby. She wanted to know if they had brought all his stuff. She made multiple trips, loading everything into her car, before she finally picked up the baby and took him away.

I was struck by her apparent lack of emotion. I didn't know the details; it would have been inappropriate for them to tell me. But this wasn't the happy reunion of birth mother and baby boy that I was expecting.

"Sometimes it happens," they said. "There are no guarantees. If the adoptive parents had sued for custody, they probably would have won. But that is a lengthy and expensive fight. Not everyone can take that on. Understand, this is one of the risks with open adoption. Now that you've seen it for yourself, is this something you still want to pursue?"

Good question. I went home and Steve and I had a long discussion about it. We sat with it over the weekend and decided we still wanted to try to adopt. We couldn't shake the feeling that God was in control and it was going to be okay.

In December 1990, I was volunteering as usual in the AO office. I took a phone call from the mother of a potential birth mom. This was the first time I had talked to a birth grandparent. That call gave me a new perspective. Until that moment I hadn't thought about anyone beyond ourselves and the baby we would adopt, and the birth mom of course. Obviously, a birth mom would be likely to have parents that were facing this difficult choice, and maybe there were even siblings dealing with this unexpected event in their family.

I talked to this grandma-to-be, giving her all the information she needed. I put together the information package as usual and stopped to mail it on my way home.

Something felt different about this one. When I went to drop it into the mail slot, my hand wouldn't let go of it. I had an overwhelming urge to pray over it first.

Now, having been raised fundamentalist Baptist, this urge to lay on hands in prayer was shocking. It simply wasn't done. That was the kind of thing that happened in liberal or charismatic churches, certainly not the Baptist church I grew up in or currently attended. I was not at all sure this was a good thing.

But as I questioned this strange impulse, the urgency grew. It was as if God said to me, "Stop arguing and just pray already!" So, I prayed. I prayed for this young birth mom who had a difficult decision to make. I prayed for her parents, that God would grant the strength and grace they needed to support their daughter. I prayed for any siblings in the home, that they would be given the opportunity to continue to be aunt or uncle to this new life. I prayed for the couple that would be chosen to raise this baby, that God would bless them with grace and wisdom. And I prayed for the baby, that God would give them a wonderful life, and that they would know how much they were loved by everyone involved.

When I finished, the envelope slipped easily from my fingers into the mail slot. It was the strangest spiritual experience I ever had. I didn't know what to think, except that whenever that encounter came to mind, I would pray again for that baby and his or her extended family.

27

Meeting the Birth Grandparents

JANUARY 26, 1991. I WAS volunteering at AO. I was informed that a potential birth mom was coming in, but her situation was unique. She was from out of town and she had to accomplish in one day what usually took at least three visits. She was coming in with her parents, who would be waiting in our offices while their daughter completed the required videos and appointments and paperwork.

I would be allowed out to use the washroom or to make coffee, but even then, I wasn't to interact with the clients. This turned out to be a challenge.

When they arrived, the birth mom walked into the back office to check in. Oops. Nothing I could do about that, except be sure to not address her or make eye contact. The facilitators ushered her back out to the main area as quickly as they could.

It was impossible not to see her—she was so cute with her belly and glasses and big smile! It was obvious from her advanced pregnancy that she didn't have much time left to make arrangements. It was no wonder she had to fast-track everything and do it all in one day.

I kept busy with a new database, updating client files. I did eventually have to use the washroom, and I made a fresh pot of coffee for the parents while I was at it. I knew I wasn't supposed to talk to them, but that was impossible. They were so friendly and asked questions about who I was and what my job entailed. I wanted to be polite, but I also knew I was breaking the rules.

After a few hours, the facilitators came back to talk to me. They had a couple questions about our file. Could I give them a bit more detail about a few things? I thought it was a little strange, but they made some excuse and I didn't think much of it, until they came back with another question. And then another one.

"Ok, what's going on?" I asked.

"Don't get too excited," they said, "but the birth mother is down to choosing between two files, and yours is one of them."

My heart was in my throat. "What do I do? Do I call Steve? He's in Vancouver on business."

"There's nothing you can do except wait and see," they said. "Just try to keep busy with the data entry you are working on. Answer the phone as usual. We will update you when we can."

Time slowed to a crawl. It was impossible to focus on my work. I made so many mistakes with my data entry that I finally gave up on it entirely.

After what felt like an eternity, the facilitators came to me and told me that our file had been chosen. We were matched with this birth mother. I was reminded that anything could happen. She could change her mind at any time. But things were going to happen quickly because she was due in four weeks.

Also, the birth mom wanted her parents to meet me. She didn't want to meet me yet, because she didn't want to like me and then feel bad about disappointing me if she changed her mind after the baby was born. But she trusted her parents' opinion, so while she watched a couple of informational videos, I met her parents.

It was time to call Steve. It took a couple calls to his local office to get the number of the office where he was in Vancouver. I insisted it was an emergency, and they finally found him and interrupted his meeting.

While I was on the phone with Steve, explaining to him that our file had been chosen, the birth mom's dad came into the back office. He walked right up to me, gave me a huge hug, and said, "Congratulations! You're going to be a mommy!"

I had no idea how this introduction would go, but I was completely unprepared for that! He picked up an extension, congratulating Steve on becoming a dad. After the call with Steve, the facilitator suggested we all go down to the basement café, get some coffee, and get to know each other.

I felt nervous and excited and afraid all at once. I just hoped that I wouldn't say anything to screw it up. I felt a great deal of empathy for this couple. They were near the age of my oldest sibling. They were expecting their first grandchild, but none of this was going the way they had imagined.

My heart broke for them, and I told them so. "I can't imagine what you are going through. This can't be how you expected to become grandparents."

The tears flowed and our hearts knit together. They wanted to know more about Steve and me—where we came from, our families of origin, how we met, how we ended up in Winnipeg.

I felt immediate and deep affection for them, and they seemed to feel the same. They were confident that their daughter had made the right choice. They shared that the day before they had phoned in a prayer request to *Focus On The Family* for their daughter as she chose parents for her baby. They told me they felt like their prayers had been answered.

28

Becoming Parents

THERE WERE SO MANY THINGS to do to prepare for this adoption, and only four weeks to get it all done. I have never been a list maker, but suddenly I was making lists for everything. I even had a list to keep all my lists organized.

Steve and I were cautioned not to tell anyone. Anything could happen—the match could fall through at any time. As painful as that would be, it would be even more painful to have to un-tell everyone we told.

The main rules were:

- Don't tell anyone.
- Don't buy baby furniture.
- Only buy what was needed for the diaper bag to get the baby from the hospital to temporary care.
- Get a lawyer.

Steve's extended stay in Vancouver allowed him to fly home every second weekend or me to fly there. The weekend after we were matched with a birth mom, I flew to Vancouver so we could spend the weekend making plans.

We needed to choose first and second choice for baby names, for boy and girl. I picked up a baby name book in the airport. We spent hours selecting and discarding names—I must have thrown the book away at least three times.

We knew we wanted three names—the first would be a name unique to the baby, the second and third names would represent the birth family and the adoptive family. We asked our facilitator to ask if there were any family names from the birth family that we would be allowed to use. We finally came up with four name options, two boy names and two girl names.

We were responsible for packing a diaper bag to send to the birth mom, loaded with all the essentials needed to get the baby from hospital to temporary care.

We drove across the border into Washington State to an outlet mall. We

This was the cure for all my pain and sadness. Finally, being a mommy would make it all better.

found a department store and hit the baby section. Most of what we needed I would buy in Winnipeg—bottles, onesies, receiving blankets, diapers. In Washington, we were looking for a going-home outfit. We didn't know if the baby was a girl or a boy, so the outfit had to be gender neutral.

We found a white velour sleeper with baby bunny ears on the hood and a puffy tail on the bum. We fell in love with it. We did wonder if the birth family would think we were nuts, dressing the baby up like a bunny, but we decided to take the risk. The outfit was just too cute.

I packed up the bag and sent it off, hoping the birth mom would have fun going through it and seeing everything we had chosen for the baby.

And then we waited. It felt like forever. I wondered how women who had to wait through an entire gestational period managed it—were they as impatient as I was?

I mean, this was it for me. This was the cure for all my pain and sadness. Finally, being a mommy would make it all better. I know now no baby should be born with a job. It is not a baby's job to fix anything. A baby can't keep a struggling marriage together. A baby can't cure loneliness or fix depression. But all I knew was the intense desire to be a mommy, and having a baby was my best hope of climbing out of my depression once and for all.

Our baby girl was born and in my arms at last! However, our new baby wasn't the magic wand that made all things better.

I wasn't prepared to feel grief over our birth mom's and her family's loss. Relinquishing a child for adoption, even open adoption, exacts a terrible price of grief. I discovered, alongside my intense joy, I also felt the sharp pain of loss deep in my soul on behalf of our birth mom. Driving away from her house with her/our baby broke me.

I wasn't prepared for the crippling fear of suddenly becoming a parent and all the responsibility that would now weigh on my shoulders for the rest of my life. I was a mess, however well I covered it up most days. What if I totally screwed up this kid? What if I was lying to myself that this was all God's will so it would all be fine? Was I just seeking to fill my selfish desire for a baby? If I messed this up, I wasn't just messing it up for us and this child—I was destroying the hopes and dreams an entire birth family carried for this child. Could I live up to those expectations and be a perfect mom under that kind of pressure? I wasn't prepared for the kind of sleep deprivation a newborn baby brings with them. I mean, even when I was sleeping, I wasn't fully sleeping. I was listening for all the little snorts and snuffles coming from my precious newborn.

I wasn't prepared for how hard it was to leave our baby daughter overnight at our temporary care home the law required her to stay at for a ten-day waiting period during which the birthmother could revoke her consent to adopt. I felt like I couldn't breathe when I wasn't with her. We stayed until her last feeding, around 11pm, and were back again by 7 am. Those poor people—dealing with us coming and going at those hours must have been exponentially more difficult than those ten days of getting up in the middle of the night for her bottle.

I wasn't prepared for post-adoption depression, which is the adoptive mom's version of postpartum depression. Especially in 1991, it was much less talked about than postpartum depression, which also wasn't talked much about. The supposition, which I also held, was that I would have no good reason to be depressed now that all my dreams of building a family had come true. I didn't factor in the toll that pre-existing stressors like infertility and the resultant relationship struggles can take on a person's mental health, not to mention whatever baggage we bring to parenting as a result of how we were parented.

My depression plummeted to a new low. I was experiencing typical sleep deprivation. Steve was busy at his job. He was only given two weeks of paternal leave, and that went by way too quickly. Before I knew it, he was back to working 12-hour days, sometimes longer, and I was alone with a newborn who didn't feel like mine yet. It felt like the babysitting job that never ended.

Most days it was a struggle just to keep up with making bottles and doing baby laundry. When Steve had to travel for work, which was often, like two to three weeks out of every month, most of the time I didn't even bother to get dressed. I spent most of my time in my bathrobe, wondering when the happy would magically kick in.

I loved my baby—Brittany brought me so much joy—but I didn't recognise this person I was becoming. I could manage the few times a week I had to show up at church and interact with others, showing off my beautiful new baby, and fielding stupid questions like "Does she look like her real mom?"

We were renting our house from church friends who were on a northern work assignment for a couple years. One day they showed up at the door unannounced. That was not one of my better days.

I was in my bathrobe in the middle of the afternoon. The house was messy. The garden hadn't been weeded. My friend was furious.

It was obvious I wasn't taking care of their home to her standards. She was angry and disappointed. That was the beginning of the end of that friendship.

It's easy to judge me for my inept homemaking. It's easy to judge her for reacting with anger instead of compassion. She could have asked if I was okay, but that just wasn't done then. That kind of insight and compassion was extremely rare, especially in our church culture. There were high expectations, and I wasn't meeting them. It was as simple as that.

The nightmares continued, only now there was a more sinister element to them. The new theme was my baby was in danger, and my siblings wouldn't let me rescue her, and laughed when I cried and begged for their help.

But there were also some really lovely days that fed my hope during that time. The days I got to spend with our birth mom, and sometimes her family too, were so special. Our open adoption, which had started with pictures and letters, was growing into something unique and precious. Brittany's birth family treated us like family. In fact, they taught me how to be part of a family that loved and accepted me for me, with no other agenda than mutual love and respect.

They helped me to learn how to do family in a new way. I learned that family is more than shared DNA. I learned that I could make room in my life for new family relationships. And I learned how to start managing my expectations of people.

I made space for those who wanted to develop deep relationship with me.

I invested heavily into those relationships. Those individuals remain in our immediate family structure and our kids still benefit from those connections.

I still had regular contact with my family of origin, but it became obvious over time that I was the only one reaching out to connect. I called my mom regularly, of course, and we drove to visit as often as we were able. It was important to us that our daughter knew her grandparents.

It was a good eight hours' drive to my parents' house, but we did it when we could. We always left with an open invitation to everyone to come visit, and two of my siblings did come for a weekend before we became parents. I do appreciate that they made the effort at the time.

I had hoped becoming a parent would elevate my status in my siblings' eyes. I don't know if it did or not. I mean, my whole life was about doing everything differently from my eight preceding siblings and choosing open adoption certainly qualified. I was just different and that wasn't going to change. So, I learned to manage my expectations of my family of origin. I accepted that my definition of meaningful relationship was different from theirs, and that was okay. I remained kind and respectful, but I saved my relationship building efforts for those who were interested in making the same effort with me.

My mom was worried about me still feeling like an outsider in the family, and rightfully so, because I did still feel that way. Years later, when she became ill with leukemia, I went to stay with her a couple times. It was more difficult for me since we were living in Calgary then, and it had become more complicated and expensive to visit.

Once when I was there for a number of days, she shared with me her fear that the bond between the siblings wouldn't be as strong once she was no longer there. She knew that the family gathered for her sake, and she was worried that would change once she was no longer there to provide a reason.

I tried to put her fears to rest. "Of course, they are still going to get together. You don't have to worry about that, Mom."

"You said they," she said. Nothing got past her.

I think we both knew that although she didn't like it, it was what it was, and it wasn't changing now. We didn't talk about it any further. I didn't see the point in upsetting her over something over which she had no control.

29

Adoption #2

A COUPLE YEARS AFTER BRITTANY was born, we decided to reactivate our adoption file and try for another baby. This news was met with great enthusiasm from her birth grandparents. They were loving being Memere and Pepere, and at the time we were their only hope of more grandbabies. We told them we had reactivated the file, so it was time to start praying! We all prepared for a longer wait since our first adoption happened unusually quickly.

We experienced two failed matches this time around. We knew this was common, but it didn't make the roller coaster of emotions any easier. Our faith that God would provide the exact right match for our family made the wait and the uncertainties easier to bear.

What didn't help was the pressure we were getting from our 4-year-old. A classmate at preschool was excited about their mommy having a baby brother or sister in their tummy. Brittany was not impressed that our tummies didn't work to make babies. "In our family," I explained, "we ask Jesus for our babies. That's how we got you. You grew in your birth mom's tummy and that's how we all became a family."

This was a familiar story—she knew all about her adoption. There had never been a day that she wondered where she came from. The names of her birth family were among her first words. She felt secure and loved, but she also felt like she was missing out on something and she wanted a baby sister.

"Fine," she said. "I'll ask Him."

She went to her room and knelt by her bed and made her request. And nine months later we had a new baby girl in the family. Seriously—it was almost nine months to the day of Brittany's prayer that Adrianna was born.

Brittany was thrilled. She loved our new birth mom. She couldn't wait to be a big sister. Again, we weren't supposed to tell people we were matched, but it was kind of impossible to keep it a secret with our 4-year-old telling everyone she knew!

Adrianna was born in the same town and hospital as Brittany. Our birth mom had already met Brittany's birth mom and birth grandma. She was comfortable with them, and even allowed them to visit her in the hospital when Adrianna was born. They got to hold my baby before I did! That felt a little unfair, but I was so happy that they were connecting. We wanted our new birth mom to understand that her baby was being welcomed into a strong family system and we would welcome her as well, in whatever capacity she felt comfortable.

The day Adrianna was released from the hospital, her birth mom brought her to us at Brittany's birth grandparents' house. Steve and Brittany and I had moved in with them for the 10-day temporary care period. This time we didn't have to leave our new daughter every night. Brittany had a wonderful time with her aunt and uncle, and playing in Memere and Pepere's hot tub every night after supper.

Birth mom came over often during that time to see Adrianna and spend time with us. Her mom came out for a few days. They took Adrianna back to where they were staying one afternoon. I wasn't worried—I wanted them to have that time alone with the baby. It was important they spend the time they needed saying hello, so they could say goodbye when it was time for us to take her home with us.

I was concerned about the age difference between our girls, but it actually worked out really well. When Brittany went to preschool every day, I had lots of one-on-one time with Adrianna. She was a snuggler and I was enjoying every moment of our cuddle times.

I didn't experience the same kind of post-adoption depression that I had the first time around. I was familiar with adoption proceedings, and Steve wasn't traveling as much. Adrianna took longer to start sleeping through the night, but we had a friend living with us at the time, and she was very helpful with night feedings on the weekend, so I managed my sleep deprivation a bit better.

There were cracks in our marriage, however, and they were becoming more obvious by the day.

30

Separation and Reconciliation

STEVE AND I WERE EMOTIONALLY disconnected. My entire life was focused on being a mom. He had been unhappy for awhile, and I just didn't notice. Our relationship became increasingly more difficult. Our friend moved out because of the tension. By the time Adrianna was six months old, I was desperate. I didn't know what to do or how to ask for what I needed, and

---

I had just pulled the pin on a hand grenade and lobbed it at my marriage, hoping for the best.

neither did Steve. One Sunday afternoon I reached a breaking point.

I packed up myself and the girls and called my nearest sibling and their spouse, asking if I could bring the girls for a week. I couldn't take it anymore, and I needed to get away for awhile to figure things out. They were kind enough to agree.

I loaded the car and went to the basement where Steve was watching football. I told him I was leaving to go to my sibling's, and if he wanted to say goodbye to his daughters now was the time. He was shocked, but he didn't ask me to stay. He went outside to kiss the girls goodbye, and I drove away with them, wondering if I was doing the right thing, terrified by what I was setting in motion, but unable to come up with a better idea. I had just pulled the pin on a hand grenade and lobbed it at my marriage, hoping for the best.

At the end of the week, he didn't want me back. While I had known that could be a possibility, I didn't have a follow-up plan. My sibling wisely made arrangements for Steve to come and get us. We were not their responsibility, and Steve needed to take us home.

However, when we got home, we decided to separate. Steve moved to the basement since we couldn't afford to rent a second place. We started counseling with the intention of navigating co-parenting while we considered divorce.

My mental and physical health was the worst it had ever been. Adrianna's adoption wasn't finalized yet and there was a very real threat of losing her. The stress made me so sick I was unable to keep food down most of the time. Sometimes I was so ill I had to go to Emergency so they could get the vomiting to stop. I was there often enough that they started fast-tracking me for emesis treatment—one injection of Gravol directly in the hip, another one in the IV, followed by one or two more IV injections was what it usually took to stabilize me.

I finally saw my doctor and was assessed for depression. I was 10/10 according to his assessment tool. He spent some time on the suicide questions—it was obvious he was very concerned about my mental wellness, especially with small children to care for.

I started taking anti-depressants. This was a very big deal in 1996 fundamentalist Baptist church culture. Prayer was supposed to fix everything.

I made the mistake of telling my mom I had started taking anti-depressants, and that our therapist wasn't a pastor. In fact, he wasn't religious at all—he was an atheist. A family member offered to pay for long-distance counseling with a pastor of their choice if I would promise to flush the drugs down the toilet. I was already struggling with medication stigma, and the offer of a dial-a-pastor didn't help.

I was struggling with a great deal of stigma about my life. My inability to get pregnant, choosing private open adoption, my failing marriage—all these things made me feel even more on the outside of my family of origin. And now I was being treated like I was scoring crack cocaine on the street instead of being supported for taking meds that were literally saving my life.

But even during the worst time of my life, there was hope. I leaned heavily on my friend who had previously lived with us, and on Brittany's birth mom, who had become a sister to me. Those women were there for me. They dropped and ran to me whenever I needed them. I would not have survived without them. They were, and are forever, my heart sisters.

They kept me going for one more day when I thought I couldn't. They took me out to play pool. They let me vent for ten minutes, and then it was time to talk about anything but my failed marriage. They showed me I could still laugh. They showed me that even if the worst happened and I became a single mom, I would be okay and they would still be there for me. They were proud of me for going to the doctor and asking for help. They encouraged me to continue therapy and keep taking my meds. They offered me the safety and support of sisterhood in the middle of the war that was my life.

My meds cleared my brain fog enough for me to function. The constant nausea and vomiting diminished. I was able to eat and sleep and cope again and be the mom my girls needed and deserved. I could think clearly, make decisions, and cope with daily stresses.

Before the meds I would wake up in the morning, feeling disappointed that I was alive, feeling completely incapable of surviving an entire day of little ones who needed me to love them, feed them, and keep them safe and happy. The antidepressants leveled my moods. I felt capable instead of overwhelmed. I smiled more and meant it. I discovered joy and hope can coexist with stress and brokenness.

My therapist validated my feelings. Normalizing my pain and struggle helped me give myself grace. I understood that my reactions to my life circumstances were normal. My feelings of hurt and disillusionment and rage weren't sins, they were simply neurotypical trauma reactions because life was hard and I had been hurt. Life had been hard for much of my life, but I had made it this far, and I had hope that I would get through this too. I gave myself permission to be honest about my broken pieces. No more faking it. No more pretending.

People learned not to ask me "How are you?" because I started telling the truth. Did I make people uncomfortable? 100%. But I discovered that the truth really did set me free—free from the mask of perfection and the burden of impossible expectations. I also learned who my people were. They were the ones who stuck around to find out how I was, and kept asking, because I mattered to them. My therapist helped me understand I deserved people in my life who cared, and who stuck around when things got messy.

God worked, but not in the way I expected. When I finally broke down and asked God to do whatever it took to heal our marriage, that's when things started to change, but I didn't like what it took. I wanted Jesus Magic to make everything in my life tidy and easy and shiny and new. I wanted my husband to change his mind about divorcing me. I wanted him to go back to the Sunday School Teaching Youth Group Leader that made me look like a respectable church lady with two perfect little church kiddos. I wanted that reputation back. But that's not what I needed.

What I needed was to have my life deconstructed down to the studs. Only then could the work of rebuilding my life truly begin. I needed to rebuild authentic relationships with people who accepted me and loved me for everything I was, including my mess. I needed the same sort of authentic relationship with God. I had to learn to manage my expectations of people and let go of relationships that no longer served me. I had to learn how to be honest and vulnerable with myself and then with others. I wanted to spackle a few holes in my soul and apply a fresh coat of paint. God wanted to tear down all the walls and create something completely new. I knew there

There is nothing wrong with Christian therapists. There is also nothing wrong with seeing a skilled therapist who may not be a Christian.

was something better waiting for me if I just leaned into the challenges and changes and hung on to hope long enough.

Eventually the divorce counseling turned into reconciliation counseling. With a great deal of professional help, we found our way back to each other. A lot of people in the church world are surprised to hear that our marriage therapist wasn't a Christian. He was a name on the list that was approved by our benefits provider and he lived near us. That's it. That's how we chose him. We didn't search out a Christian counselor because we couldn't afford anything outside of our benefits. We got judged for that, but we made the right call.

There is nothing wrong with Christian therapists. There is also nothing wrong with seeing a skilled therapist who may not be a Christian.

I grew up in a culture that taught me to take all my problems to my pastor. Depending on the pastor, that's terrible advice. Seeking help from a pastor never ended well for me. Solving my personal problems is an unfair expectation of any minister. It's just not reasonable to expect a highly trained theologian to also be a skilled counselor. I mean, it can happen, but that has not been my experience.

When I needed emergency gallbladder surgery I did not ask if my surgeon was a Christian. I didn't care about that. All that mattered to me was that my surgeon and their team were qualified to remove my miscreant gallbladder so I wouldn't be sick anymore. This is how I feel about therapy. I want to know my therapist is an experienced, highly skilled practitioner that can help me with my damaged core beliefs and broken relationships. If they love Jesus, great. If not, great. Straight, gay—whatever.

I. Don't. Care.

God can still use them in my life for my good and God's purpose, and that's exactly what happened. Our atheist therapist saved our marriage.

We did the work and we keep doing the work. There is no such thing as being done with the work. Steve and I still touch base with our therapist from time to time, even after all these years. Our therapist is retired now, but he still sees a few clients on video calls, and we are beyond fortunate that we are on that list.

It's interesting to see the looks of shock and worry on people's faces when we mention we had a session with our marriage therapist. "But I thought you guys had a great marriage!"

We do, because we see our therapist regularly, whether we think we need to or not. And guess what? We always need it.

Think about it. If you have teeth, you should have a dentist. Your body needs a doctor. If you have a faith walk, you need a spiritual mentor. And if you have a brain and big feelings and trauma, you need a therapist.

31

Finding Hope and Healing

THIS FEELS LIKE A GOOD place to tie it all up with a happy little bow, but real life isn't like that. There were more big moves for Steve's various jobs. In 2007, in the space of eleven months, we moved from Manitoba to New Brunswick to Calgary. Our girls, then a young teen and a tween, were angry, and justifiably so. They acted out. I did not react well. We spent several years in conflict with our kids.

We chose a different parenting path. It was obvious that what we were doing—expecting them to be the kids that made us look like good parents—wasn't working. We took a hard look at what really mattered, and our reputation didn't make the list. We buckled in for a long hard road that we hoped would result in lifelong authentic relationship with our girls.

It was hard to change. It was hard to hear my mom's criticism, "That's not how you were raised. Who is in control in that home?"

"Mom, I want real relationship with my kids. I want their hearts, not just compliant behavior that makes me look good. I don't care about my reputation. I care that they know they are loved and they are worth doing whatever it takes to be in relationship with them for the rest of my life. Nothing is so important that it's worth the risk of losing relationship with them."

I didn't care anymore who disapproved of our parenting. The only thing that mattered to me was our family.

We tossed out the "rules" and had a family conversation about values. We agreed that our family values included kindness, honesty, and respect for one another, and that everything we did would be informed by those values. If we made a mistake, we dealt with the natural consequences of that mistake. And of course, there was a hard rule of no street drugs. I'd like to say it was smooth sailing from then on, but boundaries beg for teenagers to shove them over. To be honest, I did my fair share of pushing over the boundaries too, and I

I had so much to be proud of and I had every reason to be perfectly happy. I was miserable.

---

had to get real about my behavior and accept the consequences of losing my temper or being inconsistent.

When things got tough and we needed to reinforce the boundaries, The Talk went something like this:

> Our family has an operating system. When you stay within the boundaries of the values you agreed to, it works well. You are pushing over the boundaries and breaking the operating system. If you are unwilling or unable to work within our family's operating system, then we need to work together to come up with an alternate plan. No anger. No fighting. No one is getting kicked out. But we do need to take 48 hours and come back with suggestions.

One of our girls didn't like our suggestions. She decided to launch herself into adulthood earlier than anticipated. It went okay until it didn't, and when she needed rescue, we dropped everything and ran to her. Eventually she decided on her own values and invested in a solid plan to align herself with success.

Overall, it took several years, but our parenting plan paid off. Both of our girls are fully launched and are responsible, self-supporting, contributing members of society. They are lovely, hard-working, empathetic, wise women. They know how to maintain healthy boundaries. They know how to build healthy relationships. They are doing the work necessary to maintain their mental, emotional, and relational health. We are so proud of the incredible women they have become.

And still I struggled hard with my own mental health. My depression cycled through ups and downs. My PTSD kept getting triggered. My anxiety was getting worse. I was not stable a lot of the time. Moving around from job to job and city to city made it difficult to access therapy. Pre-pandemic, there weren't the kind of online resources we have now. I did the best I could, but my coping strategies were failing.

I withdrew a lot of the time. I spent most of my time in bed watching TV, trying to numb my brain, until I had to go out and interact with people. Then I faked it. I pretended to be fine. I dove into huge projects with a manic energy to distract myself from my misery, only to crash because I took on too much. I secretly still thought about suicide—more often than I like to admit.

I had managed to stay married for over 30 years. I had raised two amazing, accomplished daughters. We were finally empty nesters. I had so much to be proud of and I had every reason to be perfectly happy. I was miserable.

I was self-medicating with wine and mixing it with my anti-depressants. NOT a good idea. It dulled the sharp edges of my mental illnesses, but it damaged me. It damaged my relationships with my husband and my daughters. Everything came to a head during Christmas 2020. My daughters had the courage to confront me. We had an extremely uncomfortable conversation. They got real. I got real. I decided that 2021 was going to be the year of treating my mental illness and getting better.

A couple months previous, I had heard about neurofeedback from my sister-in-law, who found it to be very helpful. During a phone conversation one day, she described the relief and recovery she was experiencing, and I started to cry.

"Oh God, this is what I need. Please, can I have this? Can you make a way for this to happen?"

I wanted to hope, but hope is so scary and vulnerable. Neurofeedback sounded like exactly what I needed, but I assumed that kind of technology wasn't available in Canada. A quick internet search proved me wrong. Not only was it available in Canada, I found three clinics providing neurofeedback in Calgary. I talked to my family about it, and we all agreed that it sounded promising and I should look into it. We knew it would be expensive, but Steve is a fantastic money manager, and he was committed to find a way to make the finances work.

A few days later, Steve came to me and said, "Well, you're not going to believe this. My mom decided to give us an early bequeathment."

"Did she tell you she was going to do that?" I asked.

"No. She just decided to do it."

We looked at each other with wide eyes.

"So we can afford for me to do neurofeedback?" I asked.

"We can afford it now. Make the appointment."

When I walked into Neurvana Health for the first time, I was nervous. I wasn't sure what to expect, but I was impressed by the calm welcoming atmosphere. The individual who took me through the stages of testing was

160

kind and professional.

There are several steps to comprehensive brain mapping.

First, I was ushered into a dimly lit office which contained a desk with a computer and testing equipment, and a comfortable chair facing a flat screen. I sat in the chair and the technician measured my head in order to select the right size cap.

The cap is made of a flexible type of vinyl, wired inside, with ports, or holes, at specific intervals. Once the cap was sitting snugly on my head, she used a blunt end syringe to apply connectivity gel through the ports onto my scalp. Then a small wood dowel was inserted onto the port. She connected the wires that came out of the back of the cap to her computer, and we were ready to begin.

Because the initial appointment takes a bit of time to do correctly, she played a YouTube channel called *Visual Escape*. This particular video was a drone tour of the Shire, with music from *The Fellowship Of The Ring*. Very enjoyable. Although the guy in the sneakers and baseball cap booking it down the hobbit hill was a bit of a head-scratcher, we had fun concocting possible scenarios to explain his cameo appearance.

Once I was connected the mapping began. I sat quietly with my eyes open for five minutes, then with eyes closed for five minutes, then followed a breathing pattern for one minute. She unhooked me and took me across the hall to another office where she set me up at a computer. I was to complete twelve tasks in a maximum of 40 minutes. These were brain games specifically designed to measure things like memory, spatial awareness, patterns, etc. To be honest, I thought I'd rock this. I play brain games on my phone. I'm good at puzzles and patterns. I did okay, but I certainly didn't rock it. The better I did the harder they got. I reached my cognitive ceiling sooner than I liked.

The entire experience took a total of two hours. It was easy and comfortable. I went back two days later to meet Dr. Corey Deacon and review the results of the mapping and testing. He had two monitors pointed toward us so we could easily see the images. He went into great detail yet made it simple to understand. He answered every question and gave us all the time we needed. I learned so much.

I learned that my forgetfulness doesn't make me stupid. My brain was just wired that way.

I learned my default for seeing everything negatively wasn't a character flaw. Even then, I wasn't a critical person. This was what traumatic events had done to my brain. I couldn't *not* see the negative first. It took intentional effort for my brain to find the positives. I learned that this default can be reset.

I learned that my mother's anxiety and emotional distress during my gestation affected my developing brain. I was born hard-wired for hyper threat assessment. As a result, since day one I have been scanning my environment for threats of any kind, assessing whether or not I am safe. Add molestation, bullying, and physical/emotional abuse, and my child-brain really didn't have a snowball's chance in hell of normally processing any of those things.

I went for neurofeedback brain training twice a week. Each time I wore a cap with electronic leads, often two different caps per treatment, depending on what they were targeting at any given time. The technician would monitor the treatment and my responding brain waves, adjusting as needed. I just sat and knitted dish cloths and watched YouTube videos. I watched all the Brené Brown TED Talks, then I watched everything they had on brain science and neurofeedback. It was fascinating and I learned a lot. The technicians were incredibly kind and very skilled at their job. I found myself looking forward to my brain training sessions, if only to see the girls at reception and visit with my technicians, all of whom began to feel like friends.

My second brain map, less than two months later, showed complete healing of my old concussion and marked improvement in my amygdala function. It took about three months for me to realize I was feeling better. The overall improvement of my mental health, especially the depression, anxiety, and PTSD, steadily continued.

God is in science.

Just like God is in my heart, God is in my mind. Just like God is the foundation of my faith, God is the foundation of science.

Prayer is a real conversation with the Creator. And I have a picture to prove it.

I went in for my last brain map to check the progress of my neurofeedback brain training. The tech and I were chatting away. He was one of my favorites at Neurovana Health. We had interesting conversations about brain science and meditation. He was telling me about research he had read about monks, who spent several weeks at a time meditating and had their brains mapped and how those results were compared to brain maps of "normal" people. The monks' brain waves were markedly different.

"Whoa!" he suddenly exclaimed.

"What?" I asked.

"This is amazing. I've only ever seen this in a book about those monks. I have to screen grab this. What were you thinking just now?"

"I was thinking about how thankful I am for this opportunity to access real healing. I was experiencing intense gratitude and saying thank you to God," I explained.

"This is what it looks like when God says, 'You're welcome.' Want to see it?"

"Yes please!"

"See that part under the 'Awakens' tab at the top of the picture, where the brain waves on the bottom reach all the way up at the same moment the brain waves at the top reach all the way down? That's what prayer looks like."

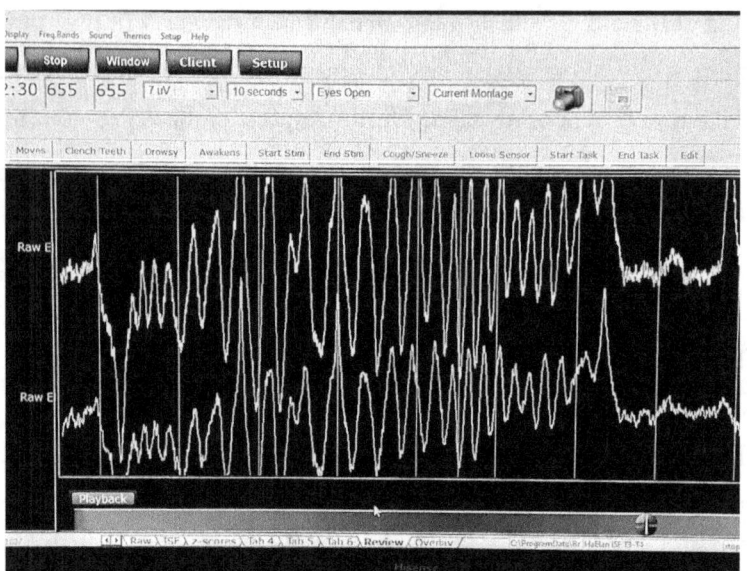

Original photo of the neurofeedback monitor screen. This is the chart that showed me what prayer looks like!

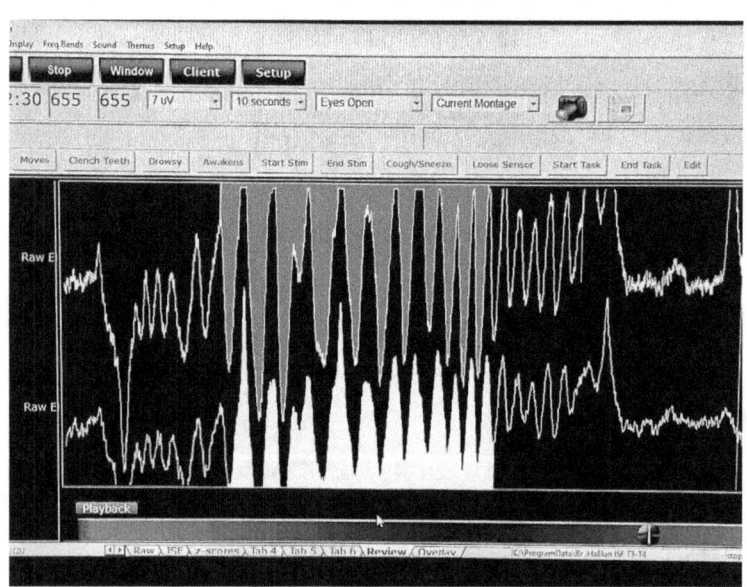

Here's the same image with the important parts of the graphs highlighted. There are two line graphs with one on top and one on bottom. They don't normally overlap like this.

At the end of six months, I was able to come off both of my anti-depressants. When I reached the point where the side effects from my medications dramatically worsened, my family doctor de-prescribed me. She cut the dosage of the first medication by half for a few weeks, then eliminated it altogether. The process was repeated for the second medication.

It gave me a great deal of satisfaction to return my unused medication to my pharmacist and say, "I don't need these anymore." Of course they didn't believe me until I told them my doctor had approved this because of successful neurofeedback brain training. They had never heard of it before, so I gave them my blog info and told them to read up on it.

At this writing I am almost two years medication free and still stable. There is no need to go back for maintenance treatments. My brain is rewired and

---

*Hope is relentlessly pursuing you
with a single-minded purpose.*

will stay that way, barring any new injuries or trauma. If I sustain a concussion or new emotional trauma I will go back for further treatment at that time.

I still notice occasional feelings of sadness or anxiety, but nothing more than any other neurotypical person would experience. I have good coping strategies. I practice healthy self-care. I have a core group of people that I can check in with when I need some extra support. Life is good, but even when it's not, it's manageable.

I am now using my story to help others. I lead a mental health ministry at First Alliance Church Calgary, called Renewing Hope, which is a 14-week facilitator-led peer support group. We work through topics including self-care, changing negative thought patterns, grief, and shame. We are intentionally creating a safe space inside church walls to talk about mental illness and trauma without shame and stigma. It is effective, it is growing, and it is healing me on even deeper levels.

That's my story. Well, most of it anyway. It's a story of trauma and kittens and mental illness and a dog and hopelessness and healing and despair and joy and marriage and kids and fear and courage and crazy and normal and ...

Hope.

I hope you see and feel the hope in my story. I hope it helps you see and feel the hope in your story. Because it's there. Hope is always there. Hope is relentlessly pursuing you with a single-minded purpose. You will collide with it, usually when you least expect it, if you just hang in there long enough for it to catch up to you.

So, keep doing that. Keep hanging in there. Lean on God. Lean on good people. Go to your doctor. Get a therapist. Find a neurofeedback practitioner near you. You can do this. You will have a story to tell to encourage the next person to hang in there until Hope collides with them.

That's a story I'd like to hear one day.

Epilogue

THIS IS A PASSION PROJECT, primarily for my nieces and nephews. They deserve to know the as-yet untold to them stories about our family.

I understand the drive to cover the wounded past and leave it behind in the annals of forgotten time. And for a time, that covering served a good purpose. But that time has passed.

A strange phenomenon occurs when the brokenness of the past is covered over for too long. It festers. It takes on a life of its own. And sometimes, it rises again as a sacred cow.

The sacred cow must be protected and served. At all costs. You have questions? You don't understand the whys of our family? The answers given to you don't make sense? Stop asking questions and fall in line.

I did not, nor do I now accept the "shut up and obey" paradigm. I kept asking questions, but I waited for the right time and learned to ask my questions in non-threatening language. And what I learned helped connect the dots. Mysteries made sense. The obscure became clear. Forgiveness and compassion flowed free and unencumbered. Shame was obliterated.

Back to the sacred cow.

This story, and more, were covered over and forgotten out of a need to protect from shame and embarrassment. I totally understand that. My parents and church leaders lived in a very different culture than we do today. Covering over those things served them and their children. For a time.

But those events never go away. They are always there, lurking just under the surface, and the threat of exposure creates fear. And the practice of covering things up, pretending they never happened, becomes a habit that leads to the sacred cow of shame and dysfunction.

It is now years later and questions rise up from a new generation. Grandchildren who have grown up and become parents want more information, not less. They grew up in the information age. They want to be the best possible parents they can be, and they are going to ask questions until they get answers that make sense. Asking why and being told "Because that's how we've always done it" just doesn't cut it for them. They keep coming face to face with the sacred cow of hidden stories of our family.

So here I am, stripping away the happy mask. The church mask. The respectable mask. I am picking up the knife of truth and honesty, and I am slaying the sacred cow of shame. Because my family deserves more. They deserve all the stories, because they can learn from them, and they can then share new wisdom and understanding and compassion to the generations coming after them.

I do love a good BBQ.

Acknowledgements

THIS BOOK WOULD NOT HAVE happened without my family, who supported my trauma recovery and mental health journey. Steve, you are my safe place and you sacrifice so much for me. You believed in me before I believed in myself. I love you and am so fortunate to be loved by you. Brittany and Adrianna, my beautiful and accomplished daughters, thank you for cheering me on. You taught me how to deep-dive into tough conversations while holding space for empathy and respect. The lessons I continue to learn from you are serving me well. I am ridiculously proud of who you are and am beyond grateful to be your mom. Adrianna, your patience while you teach me about tech and PR is nothing short of awe-inspiring. Thank you for believing I can learn new things.

Thank you to my nieces, Amy and Sarah, for reminding me that truth-telling assists not only my own trauma recovery, but others' recovery journeys as well, and that makes it worth the risk. You give me great confidence that the next generation of our family is safe in your hands.

Much gratitude to the women in my family of origin who supported this project from day one. My sister, Sue Jansma, introduced me to neurofeedback, which quite literally saved my life. Our long phone chats are always the best part of my day. My sister, Sue Davis, remains my biggest cheerleader among my siblings. That support helps me lean into deeper degrees of courageous vulnerability. My cousin, Gail Kleve, understood my need to talk about things and believes in telling the truth even when it's hard. Thank you, Gail, for filling in the gaps in my parents' story and giving me a safe place to talk.

I am so thankful for the publishing team at Siretona Creative. It takes a specific skill set to develop baby authors, and Colleen McCubbin and Charity Mongrain are the masters. Their Nestbuilder community gave me a safe place to ask all the newbie questions and learn from other authors. Thanks to all my fellow Nestbuilders for being my tribe. Extra special thanks to Travis Williams for my cover design and layout design. You made my book beautiful.

When I imagined what I wanted my cover to look like, I immediately knew I had to have an original work of art from Kyla Ferrier. Our collaboration was organic and easy, and the finished piece takes my breath away every time I look at it. Thank you, Kyla, for saying yes to my commission.

Susan Plett, you are the best editor I could have hoped for. You made this book better, and you did it with kindness and respect. You made it easy for me to feel safe with you. I still think we were twins in another life.

And a final thanks to you, my reader. You were on my heart and mind with every word I wrote. My greatest wish is that you will find pieces of your story within mine, and that it helps you access whatever new layer of growth and healing awaits you.

The Journey to the Cover Art

When I started dreaming about what my memoir, *The Ninth Child*, would look like, all I knew for sure was that I wanted cover art that was beautiful and compelling. I had a few specific elements in mind, but most of all I wanted to feel joy and freedom and light in my spirit every time I looked at it. I wanted to commission an original painting, so I needed to find an artist. Thanks to my side gig as a costume designer, I know a few people in the Calgary arts community. That's how I met Kyla Ferrier.

In 2019, I was the costumer for *Babette's Feast*, staged by Fire Exit Theatre, and Kyla played one of the leads. She kindly accepted my friend request on Facebook, and I followed her with interest when she added painting to her artistic expressions during the pandemic. I reached out to her and we started a conversation about collaborating on an abstract-representational piece that would be used to create the cover for my book. Kyla was intrigued by the idea of creating art for book covers and was eager to work with my book designer and fellow author, Travis Williams.

My concept for the art was influenced by a guided meditation with Liz Johnson at Neurvana Health, using ARDR (Audio Reflex Desensitization and Reprocessing). Liz has a lovely, calming presence, which creates a safe and welcoming atmosphere in her office. We spent some time chatting about my Adverse Childhood Experiences (ACEs) and what I could expect. Liz explained that this would be different from the regular type of talk therapy I had been used to.

Because ARDR takes a different approach, there was no need to go back to the beginning and drag up every detail of traumas experienced throughout my life. The main thing is, how have they affected me? I explained, as I often do, in a word picture.

Before neurofeedback, my place of trauma looked like a big abandoned concrete lot. It was covered in a tangle of weeds and vines and garbage that had blown in. Over time, with the help of talk therapy, I had cut through parts of it in an attempt to make a clear, safe pathway to get to the trauma in the middle. But my health benefits would run out, the therapy would stop, and it all grew over again.

Neurofeedback cleared out all of the weeds and vines and garbage, which represented my persistent severe depression. Now I had a clear, empty concrete lot, with one exception. There was my trauma, in the form of a pile of discarded scrap metal. It looked like a mound of junk, but it was, in fact, a structure of sorts, as if a group of kids had collected whatever scraps they could find, leaned all the pieces up against each other, and tried to build a clubhouse. There it sat, right in the middle of the lot. I could clearly see it, but I couldn't access it. I couldn't step even one foot onto the lot. It was as if some kind of invisible force field prevented me from doing anything except look at it from the outside.

When I described this to Liz, she handed me a pair of noise-cancelling headphones connected to a tablet. "Put these on, close your eyes, and go back to that lot. You will hear music, but I want you to focus on the lot." This would be like meditation, only instead of trying to achieve complete focus on only one thought to the exclusion of all others, I was instructed to welcome and follow every thought or experience that came along. Ask "why." Follow the rabbit trails to see where they lead. Everything in this space was there for a reason.

If I could come up with a name for the structure, that might be helpful. If not, no problem. When the music ended, I could remove the headphones.

I closed my eyes, the music started, and instantly I was transported to the lot. But this time it was different—I was able to step on to the lot and walk up to the structure. I was my child self—Little Lisa, 6 years old, wearing the dress and socks and shoes I had worn the day I was molested. I expected to feel bad, heavy vibes as I drew closer. But the opposite was true. I felt curious. I wanted a closer look. I named the structure Curious Heap.

As I came closer, a horde of cockroaches swarmed out, frantically climbing all over it. I felt fear, but it didn't belong to me. The fear came from the cockroaches. One of them scurried over to me, ran across the toe of my shoe, waved its little antennae at me, and ran back inside. All the cockroaches fled back inside as well. Then, it was as if they had conducted a meeting where the one told the rest that I wasn't there to hurt them, but they couldn't be there anymore. They all left through the bottom of the Curious Heap and ran away.

I began investigating, walking all around it. I saw the sunlight streaming in through jagged holes. I saw one big dandelion growing out of the base, and more baby dandelion leaves sprouting from between the cracks. I explored my way around to the front again and noticed there was a door. I opened it, stepped inside, and realized I had been there before.

When I was molested at age 6, I worked diligently to make myself forget. I had succeeded until the memory flooded back when I was 23. That was when I got a vision of my 6-year-old self, shackled by my ankle to my little rocking chair in a dark abandoned shack. There were holes where the sunlight streamed in. I could hear children laughing and playing in the meadow full of wildflowers just outside the door, but I couldn't leave. I was sock-footed, still wearing the dirty anklets that were ruined when I ran away from my molester.

When I did the work on forgiving my molester, the vision came again. This time the rocking chair was empty and the shackle was broken. I could hear my own laughter in the wildflower meadow outside the door. I saw the rocking chair with the broken shackle still attached. But this time I saw the dirty socks lying on the ground. They had been left behind, along with my shame.

I felt relief that Little Lisa was finally truly free. She wasn't carrying around those dirty shameful socks any longer. This entire place was devoid of life, abandoned, and useless. I wanted to dismantle it, and started examining it closer to see how that could be accomplished without it crashing in and hurting me. I had no idea how to begin, but I knew Liz was there to help me. I felt strong enough. I felt hope and joy. I knew this place would become something beautiful instead.

The vision changed, and instead of the Curious Heap, I saw a huge shade tree in full leaf with my rocking chair sitting in the shade at its base. It was surrounded by a fragrant field of wildflowers. I knew this place would remain as a place of hope and healing and joy for anyone who needed to come here and recover.

I shared this experience with Kyla and sent her an early draft of my manuscript. The painting she created was a perfect representation of my trauma and my healing. If you look closely, you can see my rocking chair in the shadows and my dirty socks laying on the ground as Little Lisa runs toward the sunshine with her Collie dog.

Travis Williams, my cover designer, collaborated with Kyla and me from the very beginning of the project. He created a beautiful book cover using select parts of the original art. It is deeply meaningful to me and I hope you love it too.

You can find more of Kyla's work on Instagram, @kylaferrierart. You can find more of Travis Williams's work at behance.net/traviswilliams18/projects.

Questions for reflection and discussion

I LOVE IT WHEN A book makes me feel and think about things. I also like questions that help me process those thoughts and feelings, so I decided to offer you these discussion prompts. You can reflect on your own, or discuss them in your book club, or even just between friends.

1. Did this book make you want to explore trauma recovery or neurofeedback further?
2. What are your impressions of the author's style? Did you find it engaging, or were you bored?
3. What part of this story do you find yourself continuing to think about?
4. What did you Google while reading this book?
5. Has this book affected how you see trauma, either your own or someone else's? If so, in what way?
6. What passages particularly affected you?
7. Did you see part of your story in the author's story?
8. What is the most important point the author makes in this book?

Learn More

Follow Lisa on:

- Instagram @lisamayleblanc
- Facebook @lisamayleblanc.author
- LinkedIn @lisa-may-leblanc-b26102aa
- Medium @lisamayleblanc

Visit her website to read her blog and sign up for her newsletter: https://lisamayleblanc.com

Photo Album

Me, not yet 1-year old, sitting in my rocking chair wrapped up in my favorite blanket.

Opening gifts with my dad on my first birthday.

*Me at 18 months old with my first collie, Princess,
who claimed me as her "puppy."*

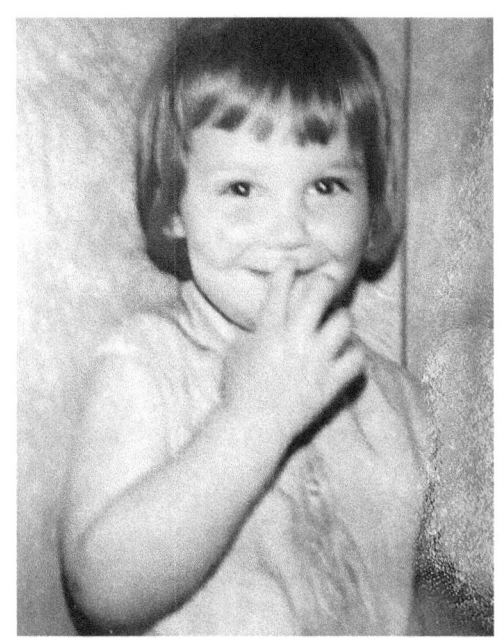

Me at 2 years old.

*Me at age 5 with my first baby doll. I already knew
I wanted to be a mommy when I grew up.*

181

*Dad had a "nap before bed" most evenings after supper. I
sometimes climbed in his lap and joined him.*

Me with my first Princess.

Me and my cousin Gordon, taken on the front porch of the farmhouse the summer I was 6. My aunt and uncle and cousins came to visit us on the farm. The boys were close to my age so we spent a lot of time playing together, which usually involved kittens.

Me at age 6, a few weeks after I was molested. My uncle was teaching one of my sisters to use his camera, as she was borrowing it for a trip. I followed them around the yard at a distance and she took this photo.

Mom and Dad knew how to have fun. This is one of my favorite photos of them.

Me at age 8. Our backyard sandbox was an old tractor tire filled with coarse sand. Something about the sand running through my fingers helped me feel calm.

Me at age 13 with Mom and Dad. Mom sewed that blouse for me—it was a favorite.

Steve and me with my parents on our wedding day, May 9, 1987.

Mom and Dad on our wedding day.

Wedding portrait, May 9, 1987

*First complete family portrait, December 1995. Brittany
was 4 1/2, Adrianna was 3 months.*

Adrianna and Brittany, December 2020 (photoHuch)

Steve and me, December 2020 (photoHuch)

Family portrait, December 2020 (photoHuch)

www.ingramcontent.com/pod-product-compliance
Lightning Source LLC
Chambersburg PA
CBHW061152120626
46546CB00005B/2033